The Right Tools

The Right Tools

A Guide to Selecting, Evaluating, and Implementing Classroom Resources and Practices

Towanda Harris

HEINEMANN
PORTSMOUTH, NH

Heinemann
361 Hanover Street
Portsmouth, NH 03801–3912
www.heinemann.com

Offices and agents throughout the world

The author and publisher wish to thank those who have generously given permission to reprint borrowed material:

Excerpt from "Improving the Instructional Core" by Richard F. Elmore. Copyright © 2008 by Richard F. Elmore. Unpublished manuscript, drafted March 2008, revised June 2008. Reprinted by permission of Richard F. Elmore.

Figure 3.6: Excerpt from *Better Learning Through Structured Teaching*, 2nd Edition by Douglas Fisher and Nancy Frey. Copyright © 2014 by ASCD. Reprinted by permission of ASCD and conveyed through Copyright Clearance Center, Inc.

Excerpt from the Common Core State Standards. Copyright © 2010 by the National Governors Association Center for Best Practices and Council of Chief State School Officers. All rights reserved.

Cataloging-in-Publication Data is on file at the Library of Congress.
ISBN: 978-0-325-10858-2

Editor: Tobey Antao
Production: Vicki Kasabian
Cover and text designs: Monica Ann Crigler
Typesetter: Kim Arney
Manufacturing: Steve Bernier

Printed in the United States of America on acid-free paper
23 22 21 20 19 CGB 1 2 3 4 5

To my husband Aaron,

our friendship

means the world

to me.

♡

Contents

Acknowledgments *ix*
Introduction *xi*

What Are My Students' Strengths and Needs?

page 1

This chapter introduces tools to help you identify what you and your students need, so that you make your own "shopping list" of what to look for in the resources you consider.

- Student Progress Tracker *3*
- Student Progress Descriptors *4*
- Student Self-Reflection Checklist *15*
- Goal Setting: Tracking Achievements *16*

How Good Is It?

page 25

The tools in this chapter will help you consider the alignment of the resources with your goals for your students.

- Resource Inventory Checklist *29*
- Unpacking the Standards *38*

How Will I Use It?

page 45

This chapter discusses how to keep the focus on our students' strengths and needs when we try a new resource.

- Grouping Planner *54*

Is It Working for My Students?

page 65

You've piloted a new resource. But is it helping your students? This chapter helps you assess how well the resource is working. It also offers guidance for keeping on track and meeting goals.

How Do I Collaborate to Learn Even More?

page 79

This chapter focuses on one of the most powerful resources available to you as a teacher: your colleagues.

- Meeting Guide *86*

Appendixes

page 93

A Student Progress Tracker *94*

B Student Progress Descriptors *96*

C Student Self-Reflection Checklist *98*

D Goal Setting: Tracking Achievements *104*

E Resource Inventory Checklist *105*

F Unpacking the Standards *106*

G Grouping Planner *107*

H Meeting Guide *108*

References *109*

Acknowledgments

My journey is one that will continue throughout eternity. When I stop learning, I stop growing. I have and will continue to cross paths with individuals who teach, encourage, inspire, motivate, and genuinely love others. I don't stand here on my own merit.

I stand on the shoulders of . . .

My partners in education. To Rozlyn Linder and Shenita Searcy, you have left footprints on the hearts of educators everywhere and have inspired students near and far. You opened my eyes to greatness. I miss you both dearly. To Salema, Alison, and Demiris, you taught me the power of TEAM. You became family.

My village. To Aaron, Keith, Joshua, and Jaden, you give me the courage to stand tall in spite of my fears. You challenge me to push forward. To mom and dad, you were the first to teach me the value of education. Your sacrifices for our family continue to open doors in my life. To my siblings, you never let me settle, even when I tried. To Karen, David, and Nicole, you always cheer for me from the stands, the sidelines, and even on the field. To Nicole Lester, your resilience and faith is an encouragement that helps me press on and advocate for all students. It means so much. To the members of the Midtown Bridge Church, you exemplify a servant's heart.

My colleagues. To David White for the valuable conversations and pulling out the welcome mat to support me in my quest to make my path in the world of education. To Melanie, you're always there to support me in my educational endeavors. Thank you, friend.

My education. To the professors in the School of Education at Clark Atlanta University. I fight for the least of these because of your desire to make quality education available to all students, regardless of their economic status.

My students. To my former third graders at Benteen Elementary School. I grew with you, I laughed with you, and I cried with you. You taught me the value of listening, you solidified my *why*. You inspired me to be the best educator that I could be. I am so proud of each of you.

My team. To Tobey Antao, you are amazing. Your patience balanced with encouragement and sprinkled with jokes made me look forward to every conversation. Together we made lemonade out of lemons and allowed loss to inspire us to be better. Thank you for listening. To my awesome team at Heinemann: Vicki Kasabian, Monica Crigler, Elizabeth Silvis, Brett Whitmarsh (social media director), Patty Adams (production director), Catrina Marshall, Sarah Fournier, Michelle Flynn (professional development). Thank you for valuing my professional experience and allowing my voice to flow throughout each page.

All educators. My teacher's hat is always on. The journey to make education relevant, engaging, and challenging for all students will never end. Your fight will be my fight. Your passion will be my passion. Our students deserve it.

Introduction

When I was eight years old, I rearranged my entire basement into a classroom so that I could be the teacher. I had a chalkboard, a teacher desk, plenty of carbon paper, flashcards, old workbooks, and anything else that I could find that looked like it might belong in a classroom. During family visits, I managed to get my cousins to play along as students, even if they called me *Ms. Davis* begrudgingly. In that room, with those tools, I was a teacher.

Perhaps this story sounds familiar to you. Many of us who are now educators once played games like these. And, in my first years as a teacher, I continued to collect a lot of *stuff*. I would keep everything I could fit in my room, year to year. I used the words *resource* and *stuff* interchangeably: I had been collecting without really evaluating what I was bringing into my classroom. At the time, I saw this as building a set of tools. But how helpful are those tools if we don't know what they can do, if they're of good quality, or if they'll work for the task at hand?

As I look back on those days now, I can see just how different this idea of teaching is from the teaching I've seen make a positive difference for children. Effective teaching comes from closely attending to student needs, being mindful of their strengths, and choosing and designing instruction that meets them where they are and moves them ahead. Early in my teaching career, I had the privilege of learning this lesson from mentors and colleagues. Later, in my work as a coach, and now on the district level, I can still see this pattern at work. Although resources have the potential to be a great help to us, having a room full of supplies doesn't make us teachers: helping our students learn and grow does.

Today, we often find ourselves facing a dizzying array of materials and resources, whether they be a box of dusty skills cards handed down from a retiring teacher, a professional book passed on by a colleague, a unit plan saved from a previous year, a teacher's manual found in the back of a storage cabinet, a procedure recommended by a supervisor, a program required by a district, a book reviewed on a blog, a set of activities discussed on Twitter, a chart found on Pinterest, a unit downloaded from a website, or a strategy highlighted in a brochure or an email. But how do we know which of these will help the children in our classrooms? How do we find helpful new resources without squandering funding or instructional time?

Or maybe we find ourselves working with the same resources we've used for years, following their guidance, yet watching students hit the same predictable frustration points. How can we make adjustments to resources to maximize our support for our students? Or do we need new resources or approaches altogether?

Or maybe we are working with resources that, for whatever reason, have come to dictate what we do in the classroom, even if they aren't meeting our students' needs. How can we take a step back from the resources' suggested plans and timelines and, instead, use them strategically to best support our students? Or how can we bring in supplemental resources to help our students?

Resources are, of course, only a piece of our work, alongside our knowledge of best practices, our understanding of our students, and our ability to work with and learn from our own team of colleagues and mentors. Yet each of these pieces can have powerful effects. When we use a resource that's well matched to our students and their academic goals, we can make strong progress. But a resource that is not a good fit can do damage by wasting time, stalling student progress, disengaging students, frustrating struggling learners, or boring advanced learners.

This can feel like many options to weigh. But, in fact, the process becomes much simpler when we keep a tight focus on the most important factors in the classroom—our students' strengths and needs. When we invest some time in getting to know these variables, it becomes easier to decide which resources and approaches to try and to see a clear path ahead. The aim of this book is to provide tools to help you make this happen.

How Can This Book Help?

This book lays out a path for identifying what you are looking for in classroom resources, gives criteria for considering specific resources, offers ideas for how to put the chosen resource(s) to use strategically, and provides suggestions for assessing whether the resource(s) are working. Each of the chapters answers a guiding question.

Chapter 1: What Are My Students' Strengths and Needs?

Think about the difference between going grocery shopping when you have a list and running into the store without a plan when you're already hungry. You're more likely to come home with what you need—and only what you need—when you've planned in advance. This chapter introduces tools to help you to identify what you and your students need, so that you make your own "shopping list" of what to look for in the resources you consider.

Tools in this chapter:

- The **Student Progress Tracker** helps you to identify students' strengths and needs and to monitor their progress across the year.
- The **Student Progress Descriptors** can help you use your observations about students to identify their strengths and needs.
- The **Student Self-Reflection Checklist** and **Goal-Setting: Tracking Achievements** involve students in their own learning.

Chapter 2: How Good Is It?

Many resources can look impressive at first, but how well do they work for the students in your classroom? The tools in this chapter will help you to consider the skills the resources support, the options they offer you as a teacher, and the alignment of the resources with your goals for your students. Additionally, the chapter discusses what "research-based" really means and includes questions to consider when examining research-based materials.

Tools in this chapter:

- The **Resource Inventory Checklist** enables us to compare resources in an apples-to-apples format.
- **Unpacking the Standards** helps us to identify the specific skills the standards require students to master.

Chapter 3: How Will I Use It?

Even if a resource comes with detailed instructions, it's still up to us—the educators who know our students best—to decide how to use it best for our students. This chapter discusses how to keep the focus on our students' strengths and needs when we try a new resource.

The tool in this chapter:

- The **Grouping Planner** connects the choices you make about instruction to how those choices will benefit your students.

Chapter 4: Is It Working for My Students?

You've piloted a new resource. But is it helping your students? This chapter discusses how to use checkpoint assessments and feedback to assess how the resource is working. It also offers guidance for keeping your class on track to meet their goals.

Chapter 5: How Do I Collaborate to Learn Even More?

No matter how well prepared we are for our work, collaboration can help us to support our students even better. This chapter focuses on one of the most powerful resources available to you as a teacher: your colleagues.

The tool in this chapter:

- The **Meeting Guide** provides a structure for drawing on your team's strengths and identifying actionable outcomes.

At the close of each chapter are guiding questions to start conversations with colleagues, instructional coaches, administrators, and other teachers as we consider what to look for in resources and approaches. These guiding questions help bring the focus back to students as we search for the right tools to meet their needs from year to year.

Full-size reproducibles of the eight tools found in the appendixes can be downloaded from *The Right Tools'* product page on Heinemann's website (click on Companion Resources): hein.pub/righttools

What Are My Students' Strengths and Needs?

Walking into a classroom for the first time can cause a whirlwind of thoughts to whip around in your mind. There are so many factors to consider about the success of your students in that school year. Outside of academics, you have to consider parental involvement, student behaviors, administrative support, and, of course, resources. I would love to share the story of how my summer preparation was the same year to year. I would

love to say that my reading corner was organized the same each year. I would love to say that classroom arrangements stayed the same throughout the year. In my "Disneyworld" I could just unpack my labeled containers and unroll my anchor charts and quickly begin teaching, day one. My reality was very different. I recall changing things up midyear because my students were not thriving. As tough as that was, I knew ultimately this was the best decision for my students. I'm sure you know this feeling. Just as businesses consider their customers when creating new products, we consider our students when developing our plans of action each year.

If your classroom is like the classrooms where I have taught and coached, you'll find a range of students, from those who are working several grade levels below to those who are working above level. The only way we can equip our students for success is to meet them where they are, and the only way to do that is to get to know their needs and strengths.

Knowing our students helps us to choose the most useful resources for them and to make every moment of our precious instructional time count.

But how do we know where our students are, what they are good at already, and what they need from us? In this chapter, we'll consider a variety of sources of information to help us get to know our students, whether we have already been working with our class for weeks or months or we are just reading their names for the first time on a freshly printed class roster at the beginning of the school year.

The Student Progress Tracker: A Tool for Keeping Your Kids First

Considering new materials, approaches, and techniques for your classroom can be dizzying: there are so many options! The key is keeping the focus on what the individual students in front of you need. This chapter will outline how to use data to identify your students' strengths and needs.

However, trying to keep twenty or thirty students' unique personalities, strengths, and needs in mind simultaneously is not feasible. The Student Progress Tracker (Figure 1.1) gives you a place to record brief notes about each student so that you can look across all of the available

Track students' growth using whatever data you have available: assessment scores, grade-level equivalencies, or the B/De/P/D levels. Using the same type of data across the year will make it easier to identify growth.

Recording noteworthy strengths and needs (such as *uses strategies when she does not understand what she is reading* or *uses textual evidence inconsistently*) can help you to keep a clear picture of your students' abilities in your mind. Update these notes as necessary.

Student Progress Tracker

Academic Achievement (*Beginner*–**B**, *Developing*–**De**, *Proficient*–**P**, *Distinguished*–**D**)

Name:	Reading Comprehension			Fluency			Phonics (K–2 only)			Reading Level		
	Fall	Winter	Spring	Fall	Winter	Spring	Fall	Winter	Spring	Fall	Winter	Spring
	Strengths:			Strengths:			Strengths:			Additional Comments:		
	Needs:			Needs:			Needs:					
Name:	Reading Comprehension			Fluency			Phonics (K–2 only)			Reading Level		
	Fall	Winter	Spring	Fall	Winter	Spring	Fall	Winter	Spring	Fall	Winter	Spring
	Strengths:			Strengths:			Strengths:			Additional Comments:		
	Needs:			Needs:			Needs:					
Name:	Reading Comprehension			Fluency			Phonics (K–2 only)			Reading Level		
	Fall	Winter	Spring	Fall	Winter	Spring	Fall	Winter	Spring	Fall	Winter	Spring
	Strengths:			Strengths:			Strengths:			Additional Comments:		
	Needs:			Needs:			Needs:					

Student Progress Tracker

Student	Academic Achievement (*Beginner*–**B**, *Developing*–**De**, *Proficient*–**P**, *Distinguished*–**D**)									Instructional Support (*Mark all that apply*)			
Name:	Vocabulary			Response to Reading			Writing			ELL	EIP	IEP	Gifted
	Fall	Winter	Spring	Fall	Winter	Spring	Fall	Winter	Spring				
	Strengths:			Strengths:			Strengths:			Notes/Accommodations:			
	Needs:			Needs:			Needs:						
Name:	Vocabulary			Response to Reading			Writing			ELL	EIP	IEP	Gifted
	Fall	Winter	Spring	Fall	Winter	Spring	Fall	Winter	Spring				
	Strengths:			Strengths:			Strengths:			Notes/Accommodations:			
	Needs:			Needs:			Needs:						
Name:	Vocabulary			Response to Reading			Writing			ELL	EIP	IEP	
	Fall	Winter	Spring	Fall	Winter	Spring	Fall	Winter	Spring				
	Strengths:			Strengths:			Strengths:			Notes/Accommodations:			
	Needs:			Needs:			Needs:						

If a student has been identified as an *English Language Learner*, has been placed in an *Early Intervention Program*, been given an *Individualized Education Plan*, or been identified as *Gifted*, there are other faculty members who may be a resource to you.

See Appendix A for a larger copy of the Student Progress Tracker or download a printable version on the product page on Heinemann's website under Companion Resources (hein.pub/righttools).

Figure 1.1 Student Progress Tracker

data—quantitative and qualitative—at once. Begin by filling in the information you uncover as you work through this chapter. You might use the codes *B*, *De*, *P*, and *D*, as the headings on the chart suggest, to note the student's current academic achievement. If so, the Student Progress Descriptors document (Figure 1.2) offers some guidance for what each of

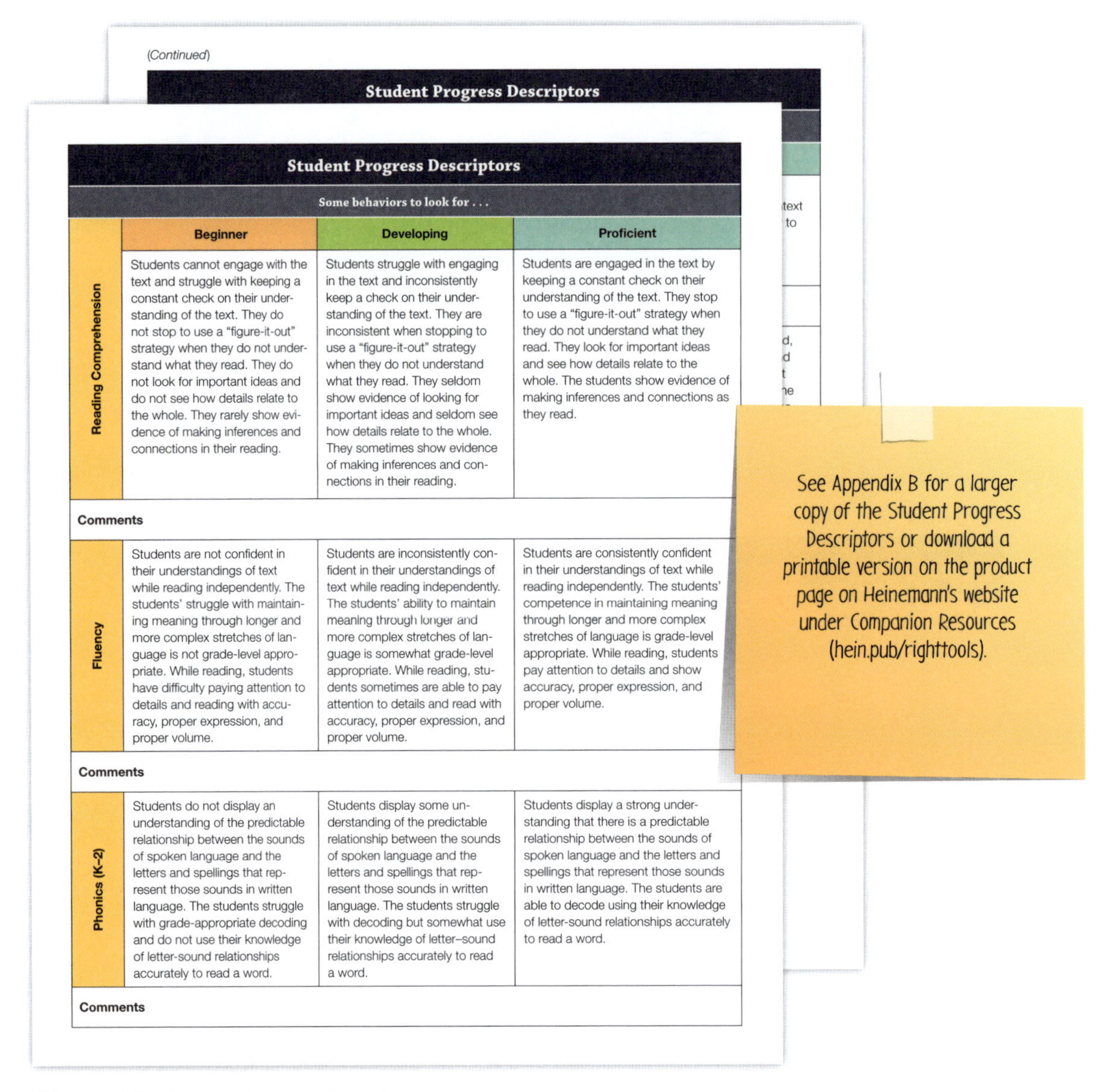

(Continued)

Student Progress Descriptors

Student Progress Descriptors

Some behaviors to look for . . .

	Beginner	Developing	Proficient
Reading Comprehension	Students cannot engage with the text and struggle with keeping a constant check on their understanding of the text. They do not stop to use a "figure-it-out" strategy when they do not understand what they read. They do not look for important ideas and do not see how details relate to the whole. They rarely show evidence of making inferences and connections in their reading.	Students struggle with engaging in the text and inconsistently keep a check on their understanding of the text. They are inconsistent when stopping to use a "figure-it-out" strategy when they do not understand what they read. They seldom show evidence of looking for important ideas and seldom see how details relate to the whole. They sometimes show evidence of making inferences and connections in their reading.	Students are engaged in the text by keeping a constant check on their understanding of the text. They stop to use a "figure-it-out" strategy when they do not understand what they read. They look for important ideas and see how details relate to the whole. The students show evidence of making inferences and connections as they read.
Comments			
Fluency	Students are not confident in their understandings of text while reading independently. The students' struggle with maintaining meaning through longer and more complex stretches of language is not grade-level appropriate. While reading, students have difficulty paying attention to details and reading with accuracy, proper expression, and proper volume.	Students are inconsistently confident in their understandings of text while reading independently. The students' ability to maintain meaning through longer and more complex stretches of language is somewhat grade-level appropriate. While reading, students sometimes are able to pay attention to details and read with accuracy, proper expression, and proper volume.	Students are consistently confident in their understandings of text while reading independently. The students' competence in maintaining meaning through longer and more complex stretches of language is grade-level appropriate. While reading, students pay attention to details and show accuracy, proper expression, and proper volume.
Comments			
Phonics (K–2)	Students do not display an understanding of the predictable relationship between the sounds of spoken language and the letters and spellings that represent those sounds in written language. The students struggle with grade-appropriate decoding and do not use their knowledge of letter-sound relationships accurately to read a word.	Students display some understanding of the predictable relationship between the sounds of spoken language and the letters and spellings that represent those sounds in written language. The students struggle with decoding but somewhat use their knowledge of letter–sound relationships accurately to read a word.	Students display a strong understanding that there is a predictable relationship between the sounds of spoken language and the letters and spellings that represent those sounds in written language. The students are able to decode using their knowledge of letter-sound relationships accurately to read a word.
Comments			

Figure 1.2 Student Progress Descriptors

those codes might look like in real life. Alternatively, if you are tracking student achievement with particular test scores, you may want to use that data in the tracker. The goal here is not to have a beautifully filled-out tracker but to identify meaningful, current data that will help you to see patterns and growth.

You'll see that the tracker has fields for data from fall, winter, and spring. By adding data at each new season, you'll be able to see how each student is progressing. If you're working through this tracker in the fall and using data from the end of the previous year, keep in mind that students may have improved their skills or had a bit of "summer slide" since then. You'll want to double-check that data against fresh data, formative assessments, or your own observations.

Having student data gathered in one place will enable you to look across it for patterns that will help you to choose the best materials, approaches, and techniques for your students: What are the most common, most pressing issues to address? Where do you see outliers who will need either extra support or extra challenge? The tracker is also an invaluable help in grouping students (as discussed in Chapter 3). Finally, using the tracker to keep your data close at hand will help you to see if and how the new ideas and tools you're bringing to your classroom are helping your students.

The sections that follow will help you to use prior student work, input from instructional support teams, and assessment data to gain a more complete picture of each student in your class. Use the Student Progress Tracker to record quick notes about what you find. At the end of this chapter, we'll analyze the notes.

Do You Have Access to Student Portfolios or Prior Student Work?

In some of the schools in my district, we have an ongoing portfolio system: each student has an eight-tab binder, organized by subject, kept by the teacher throughout the year. At the end of the year, the teacher turns the binder over to the student's new teacher. This process helps the upcoming teacher make informed decisions based on the student's previous performance: the more data we have, the better informed our decisions will be. The system isn't perfect—new students don't have portfolios when they first enroll in the school, portfolios are sometimes incomplete, and students' skill mastery may erode somewhat during long breaks—but it is valuable nonetheless.

I realize that not every school has such a robust system. However, if you have access to *any* of your students' previous work, it may help you to get a better idea of your students' strengths and needs.

How to Use Portfolios to Get to Know Your Students' Strengths and Needs

Over the years, I have found value in the use of portfolios because they provided a snapshot of the strengths and areas of growth for my students. There are great benefits for using portfolios as a strong data point to quickly determine a great starting point for the year. Because there isn't a formula for developing portfolios each year, it can be challenging to know what's useful and what's not. As you begin looking through students' portfolios, I have identified a few questions that may be helpful to ask when determining the most useful components to find a great starting point of action.

Practice Opportunities (Student Work Samples)

- What examples show the student's areas of strength on an identified skill or concept?
- What evidence demonstrates student's misconceptions of an identified skill or concept?

Assessment

- How does the student show a clear understanding of an identified skill or concept?
- Based on this performance, what misconceptions does the student display that causes concern for his expected mastery of an identified skill or concept?

For What Special Services Are Your Students Eligible?

Classifications such as *English language learner*, *special education*, and *gifted* tell us that the district has more information on these particular students. To receive these classifications, students must be assessed, and the results of the assessment must be reported. Some districts develop action plans to meet the specific instructional needs of the students within each classification.

How to Learn More About Your Students with Special Needs

Knowing what to ask can be challenging when attempting to meet the needs of your students prior to the start of a new school year. Here are a few questions that may be helpful to ask staff members who support your students with special needs or to look for in special services documentation when planning for instruction within your classroom.

- In what learning setting is the student most successful?
    - Should the student work or be assessed in a different setting, such as a quiet room with few distractions?
    - Does the student's place in the classroom affect her learning (for example, does the student do her best work when she is near the teacher)?
    - Does the student require special lighting or acoustics considerations?
    - Should the student be assessed in a small-group setting?
    - Are sensory tools, such as an exercise band that can be looped around a chair's legs, helpful to the student to maintain focus?
- What are the student's Individualized Educational Plan's goals and required accommodations?
- What formative or summative assessments are available to determine progress of identified goals?
- What available resources have been most or least successful to support the student's learning?
- What additional services will the student receive during the school day?
- What motivation strategies best support the student's learning?

What Assessment Results Are Available?

Assessment can help us to pinpoint our students' academic strengths and needs in many ways, including:

- Providing diagnostic information that helps to determine students' readiness for new skills
- Motivating students by helping them monitor their learning and progress on identified skills

- Helping to see student transfer and application skills through different modes of learning
- Informing instructional decisions to reteach or re-expose students to content
- Providing formative information that helps to identify support needed prior to gathering summative information.

However, the term *assessment* often seems to have a bad rap, carrying a sense of judgment and dread.

I remember my student James, a boy who loved to learn. He worked well with his classmates and, when given the opportunity, would quickly step into a leadership role. He was a strong student, and his mom was heavily involved in his education. There was only one problem: he had test anxiety, and the third-grade state test was on the horizon. It was called an assessment but, in reality, it was more of an accountability check. It was used to determine students' academic readiness for their upcoming grade.

The thought of being left behind just terrified James. He was so anxious during the administration of the test that his upset stomach got the best of him, and his breakfast soiled his answer key. He had to be removed from the testing environment, clean himself up, and return later to complete the test. Needless to say, even though James had mastered the material in my classroom, he did not pass. Fear had overpowered his ability to show what he knew.

All of us who have spent time in classrooms can probably recall a story like James'—a situation in which assessment did more harm than good. Some of us may even have had experiences with assessment that left us feeling a bit like James himself did. It is up to us to make sure that we're using assessment in the best interest of our students, to make decisions that will benefit them. Both formal and informal, traditional and nontraditional, assessments help us to draw closer to identifying our students' needs and strengths.

Gather and Sort Assessment Data

Begin by collecting results from assessments that your students have already taken in your class. If it is the beginning of the school year, look for results of assessments that they took in the previous school year, such as state assessments and reading level assessments.

Now, take a step back: What kinds of assessments do you have before you? Knowing what kind of assessment you're dealing with can help you to determine what to look for in each one. Figure 1.3 gives an overview of the three basic types of assessments. Which are represented in the data you've gathered?

The more types of assessments you have in front of you, the clearer an image you can form about where your students are. Imagine picking up a letter and randomly reading a single sentence from the middle. The sentence itself will probably not mean much of anything; however, when placed back in the letter, it makes sense. In the same way, only using some types of assessments is not a very useful method: it gives you only part of the picture. The purpose of each type of assessment varies and is used to make different instructional decisions. For example, an exit ticket at the

Types of Assessments

Frequency	Quarterly or Annually	Weekly or Biweekly	Quarterly or Annually
Type	**Diagnostic**	**Formative**	**Summative**
Purpose	• Administered prior to instruction • Used to identify students' baseline strengths and weaknesses/to determine what students already know • Results are intended to inform future instruction	• Used to check for understanding throughout the year • Guides teacher decisions about upcoming instruction • Provides feedback to students about their performance • Supports teacher with differentiating instruction	• Evaluates student learning at the conclusion of an instructional period (e.g., unit, marking period, year) • Aligns with the goals and expected outcomes of instruction by the end of the instructional period • Used to identify trends across the classroom • May guide teacher's decision about spiraling missed concepts in future instruction
Examples	• Unit pretest • May be teacher designed or may be part of a program • Questionnaires	• Strategic questioning • 3-way summaries • Turn-and-talk • 3–2–1 countdown • Classroom polls • Exit/admit tickets • Discussions • Graphic organizers • Four corners concept maps	• End-of-course test • End-of-year test • End-of-grade standardized test (including state-mandated tests) • District benchmark • Common assessments • End-of-unit test • Midterm exams • Final exams

Figure 1.3 Types of Assessments

closure of a lesson would be used to inform or adjust the focus for the following lesson versus an end-of-unit assessment, which could be used to evaluate students' learning against some standards or benchmark. Similarly, summative assessments may give us an idea of skill acquisition at the conclusion of a defined instructional period, but waiting until the end of a period to see if something is working wastes precious time. To help us see efficacy day by day and to adjust our instruction to ensure that we meet students' needs, we must rely not on summative assessment but on formative assessment.

How to Use Diagnostic Assessments to See Students' Strengths and Needs

Diagnostic assessments are preassessments that help a teacher to determine students' individual strengths, weaknesses, knowledge, and skills prior to instruction—a kind of baseline measurement. Diagnostic results can be used to diagnose student difficulties and to guide lesson and curriculum planning.

Ideally, a school might use a standard diagnostic test each year, to enable teachers to look for trends in comparison to previous years or to determine trends across the same grade level. In one of my coaching roles, I worked in a school with a schoolwide assessment team, better known as the SWAT, which helped teachers to obtain useful assessments in the early weeks of school. These kinds of systems can be an enormous help, and they're worth building if they're not already in place in your own school. However, even if you're working without this kind of database or support team, you can still learn from the diagnostic test results that are available to you. Here are some helpful questions that could assist with the use of diagnostic assessments as a tool to improve students' performance:

- What primary skills or concepts does this tool assess?
- Is this diagnostic tool used as a baseline or a benchmark to identify an expected progression of skills?
- What learning goals should be set for the students, based on their performance on the assessment tool?

How to Use Formative Assessments to See Students' Strengths and Needs

Formative assessments are key to informing instructional decisions. They help us to see when we should provide additional meaningful practice opportunities for students and when students are ready to move on to a new challenge. This type of assessment is given frequently and is treated as a checkpoint: the information obtained will allow teachers to evaluate students' comprehension, learning needs, academic progress, and more. Here are some helpful questions that could assist with the use of formative assessments as tools to improve students' performance:

- What learning goals am I focusing on?
- How can the current learning goal focus provide a checkpoint (formative assessment) for the end goal (summative assessment)?
- What actions will I take as a result of the student's performance on the checkpoint, and how will that help them move closer to the end goal?

How to Use Summative Assessments to See Students' Strengths and Needs

Summative assessments are less frequent and are administered as a culmination of a course, a unit, or an academic year. These assessments assess several skills and/or standards over a designated period of time. Unlike formative assessments that emphasize feedback and instructional adjustments, summative assessments yield a final grade or score. This grade or score informs teachers of the student's learning, skill acquisition, and achievement. Here are some helpful questions that could assist with the use of summative assessments as tools to improve students' performance:

- How did frequent checkpoints inform curriculum adjustments to ensure alignment to the summative assessment?
- Was the student's performance on each checkpoint a strong predictor for the student outcome on the summative assessment?
- Based on the student's performance, how did the activities and resources provide explicit practice to impact student growth?

Using Assessment Responsibly

Assessments can be a powerful tool, but only when used purposefully and responsibly. Subjecting students to unnecessary assessments causes stress and wastes valuable instructional time. So how do we ensure that our assessments are helpful, not harmful? How do we shift this perception that some of our students, like James, who I mentioned earlier, have about assessments? First, we consider whether assessment is necessary: has a school or district assessment already provided the data we need? If so, use those results rather than retesting a student. We can stay focused on *why* we are assessing: to inform instruction. With this in mind, we use assessments when we need them, with specific goals in mind. We do not assess without a plan for how we will use the results.

We also consider how we can invite students into the assessment conversation at the beginning, clarifying why we are assessing and how assessments will *help* them. Having a snapshot of each of your students could be very helpful, but this information is not only useful for the teacher—it is equally useful for the student. When students know where they are, they have a better idea of where they need to go. Students in classes that emphasize improvement, progress, effort, and the process of learning rather than grades and summative performance are more likely to use a variety of learning strategies and have a more positive attitude toward learning.

Having regular progress talks with students and letting them set goals for themselves helps them to become active participants in their personal growth. Helping students see where they are, showing them how to grow, and helping them along the way is the best way to see improvement.

The Student Self-Reflection sheets (Figure 1.4) give you and your students a tool to identify and discuss areas of strength and areas of need. The areas for self-reflection are aligned with the whole-class tracker you've been completing in this chapter. Although it might seem easier to simply tell students what you have observed about their skills, it is more effective to confer with students individually, using the self-reflection sheet to prompt discussion about areas of strength and areas where more growth is necessary. Then, use the Goal Setting: Tracking Achievements

Student Self-Reflection Checklist

Reading Comprehension

As I read, I continue to check for understanding.				
I stop to use a reading strategy when I do not understand what I read.				
I look for important ideas and see how the details in the text relate to the whole.				
I can visualize in my head the events noted in the text.				
I can make connections to the text to make an inference.				

Figure 1.4 Student Self-Reflection Checklist

form (Figure 1.5) to set goals and to identify how students will work toward those goals. Once the goals are set, confer with individual students regularly (in my classroom, I conducted weekly conferences) to consider their progress and to make adjustments when needed.

The Goal Setting sheet is meant to be a quick snapshot of the student's achievements. It's quick, it's simple, and it allows for rich conversations between the teacher and the student. However, it is only a

Goal Setting: Tracking Achievements

What's Your *Reading* Goal?	Benchmark	Fall	Goal Met?	Winter	Goal Met?	Spring	Goal Met?

To meet my goal, I will . . .

- ______________________________
- ______________________________
- ______________________________

Goal Setting: Tracking Achievements

What's Your *Writing* Goal?	Benchmark	Fall	Goal Met?	Winter	Goal Met?	Spring	Goal Met?

To meet my goal, I will . . .

- ______________________________
- ______________________________
- ______________________________

See Appendix D for a larger copy of the Goal Setting: Tracking Achievements form or download a printable version on the product page on Heinemann's website under Companion Resources (hein.pub/righttools).

Figure 1.5 Goal Setting: Tracking Achievements

meaningful tool when it is used consistently and when we, as teachers, use the goals identified to help us make decisions about what we will teach and what approaches and resources we will use in our instruction.

Here are some guiding questions that you could refer to with students when conferring with them to set or revisit goals.

- Why do goals matter?
- What things should I think about when setting my goal?
- What motivations help me to achieve my goal?
- Who can help me achieve my goals?
- What tools do I need to be successful in achieving my goals?

Things to Consider When Creating a Goal Sheet and Discussing Goals with Your Students

- ***Be Encouraging and Positive.*** This process should done in a safe and supportive environment in which students feel comfortable with acknowledging their individual areas of growth. I used to tell my students that once the door was closed, this was our world. We built a community of learners that would cheer and congratulate each other as they reached milestones in the class. Each goal looked different, but students felt motivated to put their best foot forward to reach it.

- ***Set Priorities and Bite-Sized Goals.*** There are various factors that will support students' academic growth. It's important that you assist them in focusing and prioritizing their goals so that students aren't overwhelmed with what should be done. Too many goals can be discouraging for students, so the key is to focus on one or two at a time. I always kept in mind how skills and standards progressed throughout each grade, and it helped to inform me on the key focus areas. For example, I had a student who had a hard time with decoding, vocabulary, and comprehension. After digging deeper, I realized that when I read stories aloud to the students, his vocabulary and comprehension were strong; however, when he read independently he stumbled over each

vowel and consonant. I decided to start with decoding because that skill became an obstacle for acquiring vocabulary and comprehending the text.

- ***Be Clear About How Each Day's Work Addresses Goals.*** Helping students see their day-to-day work as steps toward reaching their goals is a challenge. There is great value in aligning each step with the overall goal of performing on or above grade level and in helping students to see how each step is part of the path to that goal. It might sound simple, but without a constant focus on where their individual instruction is headed, I have seen way too many small groups dissolve into a hodgepodge of activities.

  Naming manageable goals with students will help us in our planning, but it will also help them to monitor their own progress and ensure that they are on track. For example, students may be more interested in citing textual evidence once they realize that it is a step in helping them to meet their goal of making stronger inferences.

- ***Make Sure Goals Are Measureable.*** When teachers and students work together to track their progress in a measureable way, improvement begins to occur. Measurable goals are not subjective, and students' progress toward measurable goals can be tracked with set criteria. For example, I was working with a second-grade student on improving her fluency. The goal was broken into three parts: intonation, rate, and tone. Each lesson provided additional practice around each area. Prior to the start of the small-group lesson, we looked at the fluency benchmark for second grade. The benchmark for a midyear second grader was 100 words per minute and the student started at a score of 54 words per minute. Each week, my student read a passage in 60 seconds and we used that weekly score to determine if the goal was attainable by the end of the semester. If you're tracking progress with skills that don't yield an easy-to-calculate score, such as comprehension, try specifically naming the skills students will master. The Student Progress Descriptors rubric (Figure 1.2), models this kind of specific naming of skills.

- ***Allow Students to Take Ownership over Their Goals.*** Help students understand their role in achieving their goals. When learners are a part of the decision-making process, they tend to be more excited about their accomplishments. Creating a sense of buy-in makes the progress worthwhile. Build in reflection time for students to keep tabs on their learning. Start off each session reviewing their goal trackers and allow them to identify their "glows and grows." *Glows* are the things that the student is doing well and *grows* are the suggested areas of growth. Be mindful of the context in which we foster this mind-set: it is essential that we provide students with a judgment-free zone that is filled with praise for students' efforts and constructive feedback, not a sense of competition. Comparing students against their previous achievements helps improve their confidence in their ability to make progress. It promotes a sense of self-awareness that emphasizes self-reflection and helps students understand the relationship between their efforts and their achievements.

- ***Give Students the Instruction They Need to Meet Their Goals.*** Naming goals for students isn't enough: We also need to provide instruction that targets those goals. When I was an instructional coach, I remember working with a first-year teacher who was full of energy and ideas. The most exciting part of his day was small-group instruction. He put together colorful, bright, and engaging activities for students to do, and they loved every moment of it. I checked in with him to look at the progress that his beginning- and developing-level students were making. To his surprise they were not making nearly as many gains as they should have. We decided to analyze the work his students had been doing. He found that the activities, although engaging, weren't specifically focused on the skills his students needed to master. So, we started with the end in mind and looked closely at the activities that he was putting before students. As a result, he was able to see the direct correlation that feedback and practice opportunities had on a student's overall success. Once we know our students' needs, we are better equipped to make instructional decisions, including what resources to choose.

What Does This Tell You About Your Students?

Now that you've combed through the data you have about your students, it's time to take a step back and look for patterns.

- ***Do you have enough information?*** Were you able to gather information for all of the categories on the tracker? Are there any areas where you need more information? If so, consider how you might assess students to better understand their strengths and needs in those areas.
- ***What patterns do you see in individual categories?*** Looking at each category separately, do you notice any patterns or groupings in terms of academic achievement level? Are there particular strengths or needs that many students have in common?
- ***What patterns do you see in students' instructional support?*** Are there particular accommodations that are common to many students?
- ***Where do you see extremes?*** Are there instances in which a few students' skills seem to be far beyond or far below the rest of the class?

Next, it's time to identify what you are aiming for in your upcoming instruction.

- ***In what areas do your students need support most urgently?*** Which students need this support? Which (if any) students need more intensive support or enrichment in those areas?
- ***What student accommodations do you want to keep in mind as you consider instructional resources and approaches?***
- ***For which of these needs will you be looking for new resources and approaches?*** Which of these needs can be well addressed by resources and approaches you are already using?

Putting It into Practice

All of us who teach know that numbers don't tell the whole story; the narrative of a student's progress is much more powerful. We all have students whose stories we carry with us through our careers, and, for me, Sandra is one of those students.

She was a small, timid, and soft-spoken fourth grader who functioned on a third-grade level. As an Early Intervention Program teacher, I saw her for additional reading and math instruction a few times a week. It was challenging for her classroom teacher to truly know what she knew and which skills she had mastered because her shyness was a major obstacle during assessment time.

My class was set up like a workshop model in which stations were specifically selected to address students' individual needs. Sandra seemed to open up more in a smaller setting, which allowed me to get a better gauge of her ability level. I kept a portfolio for her that included student samples, which helped me to identify her misconceptions and gaps in her learning. Because I was looking at multiple sources of information, not just scores from a single assessment, I was able to identify the *why* and connect it to the *what*: What Sandra was doing and why she didn't grasp the material. What mistakes Sandra was making and why she was making the same errors.

Paying close attention to what I learned about what Sandra needed and what she had mastered helped me to plan what she needed to master next and what resources and approaches to try with her. Over the year, she made strong progress.

Years later, I saw Sandra again. She had blossomed into an awesome eighth grader! She ran up to me so fast and hugged me tightly. She said, "I still remember your class. You were a great teacher." It was the kind of moment that we teachers hold onto for a lifetime. But the secret of being that "great teacher" was really more about being a great *observer*: because I had learned about Sandra's strengths and needs, I was able to see a clearer picture of her academic progress, which gave me the foundation for getting her the instruction and resources she needed.

Conversation Starters

Colleagues, instructional coaches, and administrators can be valuable resources for ideas and feedback as you consider what you'll look for in resources and approaches. A few questions might lead to helpful discussions:

- Where/how can I find previous years' work samples from my students, such as an established portfolio system or work saved from the previous year's teachers?
- How could our grade (or school) work together to track individual students' progress across grades and help to inform teachers' instructional decisions?
- Is there a SWAT that can support me with gathering additional data points about each student that I support? If not, is this something that the school would be interested in developing?
- Is there a process that helps teachers get all available information on their students in one place (i.e., data tracker, data portal, shared drive, etc.)?
- I'm planning to leverage the use of individual student goal-setting sheets to plan for additional academic support for my students. What support staff might I want to talk to about setting goals for my students with special needs (i.e., special education, English Language Learners, gifted)?

Chapter 2

How Good Is It?

I vividly remember walking into my classroom my first year in education. My heart was filled with the genuine desire to make a noticeable difference in the lives of the children that I encountered. Yet, to my surprise, my college education had not prepared me for my first few years as a teacher. In college, I remember creating lessons, organizing manipulative tools, and using sentence strips for just about anything. However, in my first year of teaching, I was given prepackaged activities, workbooks, and classroom libraries. My colleagues and I were expected to use these programs "with fidelity," meaning that we were to follow them page by page. My bubble was burst, but I was determined to make lemonade out of lemons.

The first step was to look very carefully at the materials I'd been given. I soon found that I agreed with Arthur Gates, who helped to shape twenty-first-century reading instruction:

> I have always believed that if one accepts the theory that the basal reading program must be used it should be adjusted to individual needs and that each child should be encouraged to move on into wider and more advanced material as rapidly as possible. [cited in Smith 1986, 224] (Dewitz and Wolskee 2012, 1)

With this same belief, I began studying each resource from cover to cover, disregarding elements that were not helpful, keeping those that did seem helpful, and frequently customizing components to fit the needs of my students. I realized that the question I needed to ask about each component was not just "Is it good?" but "Is it good for my kids, at this point in time?"

In my work with teachers in a variety of schools over the years, I've noticed a pattern. When we don't use resources, programs, and approaches strategically, when we simply follow the path that a tool lays out for us or we stick with the methods and materials we've used time and time again, we lose sight of what our students need. As a result, students' achievement suffers, students' motivation suffers, and our sense of professionalism suffers.

I've seen this disconnect between teaching practice and students' needs in a range of schools. Here's a snapshot of one example, from a recent classroom visit. The teacher and students were completing a book study. From the outside this busy class looked great: the teachers and students were actively engaged in the learning, in both whole-group and small-group activities. But then I took a closer look. Unfortunately, the activities that students were working on seemed disconnected from the intended focus skill (determining the meanings of unknown words and phrases). At one literacy center, children were doing round-robin reading with the teacher, who stopped the reading in seemingly random places to tell students the definitions of particular words. At another center, students were copying dictionary definitions for difficult words in their book. At a third center, focused on fluency, students were partner reading, alternating by page. At the fourth center, students were working on a worksheet, answering questions about events that occurred in the book. All the activities only required students to recall and regurgitate information from the book—the very lowest level of thinking defined in Webb's Depth of Knowledge. All of these individual tools might have been useful if they had been used thoughtfully, at points when students needed the particular support they provided. However, when simply lumped together, they didn't lead to growth for students. We can do better.

In this chapter, we are going to explore three questions that are essential to empowering us to determine if a resource has the potential to be helpful to our students and, if so, to determine how to best use the resource:

- Does it meet a need that I'm not already adequately addressing with my students?
- Does it help my students meet the goals that have been set for them?
- Is there research that will tell me more about it?

Does It Meet a Need That I'm Not Already Adequately Addressing with My Students?

I remember when I first started teaching, my mentor said, "Teachers are the best thieves." My eyes grew big! She laughed and explained. She said that teachers know what's best for their kids and based on the availability of the resource, they know how to re-create, modify, adjust, and make it work for their students.

She was right, of course. Even while I was using the required program during my first year of teaching, I realized that there were best practices and strategies hidden within the pages of the materials. So like any professional educator, I began to pick and choose the strategies and routines that helped the students that I served to meet the goals I'd set for them. I carried those routines into math, science, social studies, and even health. It was great!

As educators, we're all familiar with this kind of judicious use of resources. But, as we collect resources that we trust, we need to be mindful of the overall effect of the resources we choose. It could be that our favorite resources tend to be teacher centered, giving students little time for independent practice. Or we might find that the resources we use year after year focus on introducing concepts, but that we have few supports for remediation or for mastery.

As time went on, I created a system for inventorying my trusted resources that helped me to determine the areas in which they were helping me and my students and to determine the areas in which I needed to

Roles support the "we do" stage of the lesson—they encourage students to work together and collaborate.

find additional resources (Figure 2.1). At the time, I used the required materials as my starting point, but I've found over the years that these questions are useful in considering whether any resource fills a need in my classroom.

The questions on my inventory fall into five categories, each of which is tied to a goal:

- **Stage:** ***I want my students to be able to independently use what they learned.*** To support this goal, I want to be sure that I have resources that address the stages of the gradual release of responsibility to students: "I do" (teacher driven), "we do" (cooperative work), and "you do" (independent work).

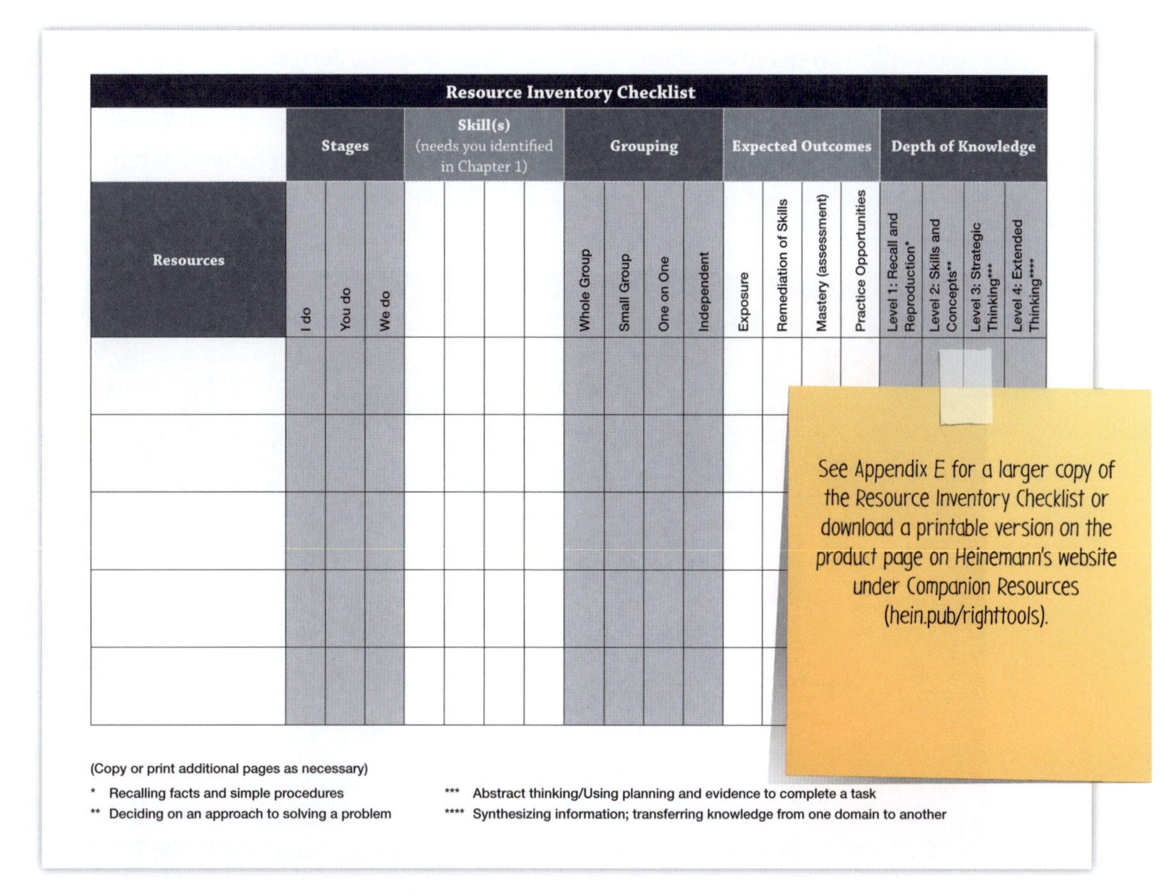

Resource Inventory Checklist

	Stages			Skill(s) (needs you identified in Chapter 1)				Grouping				Expected Outcomes				Depth of Knowledge			
Resources	I do	You do	We do					Whole Group	Small Group	One on One	Independent	Exposure	Remediation of Skills	Mastery (assessment)	Practice Opportunities	Level 1: Recall and Reproduction*	Level 2: Skills and Concepts**	Level 3: Strategic Thinking***	Level 4: Extended Thinking****

(Copy or print additional pages as necessary)

* Recalling facts and simple procedures
** Deciding on an approach to solving a problem
*** Abstract thinking/Using planning and evidence to complete a task
**** Synthesizing information; transferring knowledge from one domain to another

Figure 2.1 Resource Inventory Checklist

- **Skill:** ***I want my instruction to support students in the skills they need most.*** To support this goal, I rely on the needs I identified in my review of student data on the Student Progress Tracker (see Chapter 1).
- **Grouping:** ***I want to be sure I have opportunities to differentiate instruction.*** To ensure that I'll have these opportunities, I identify the grouping configurations that each resource accommodates: whole group, small group, one-on-one, and independent work.
- **Expected Outcome:** ***I want to be able to support my students wherever they are.*** To do this, I need a range of resources to expose students to a skill, remediate, assess mastery, and provide opportunities for practice.
- **Depth of Knowledge:** ***I want my students to be working toward greater levels of complexity in their work.*** To move them ahead, I need to provide an appropriate level of challenge for where they are at the moment, and plan to progress them to levels of greater challenge.

The criteria on your list may look different depending on your goals for your students. The important thing is that we look carefully at what our approaches and materials are actually supporting.

Search Tools (How to Get a "Great Find")

This book is devoted to helping you decide which resources are best for your students. But how do we find potential resources in the first place?

At times, we may feel bombarded by options. During my own visits to educational conferences, for example, I've felt overwhelmed walking into to the vendor gallery—so many educational resources, freebies, and demos occurring at one time. The vendors' goal was to make a sale, by any means necessary. For me, the challenge was trying to figure out the useful resources, before the last day of the conference. Needless to say, I ended up walking myself clear out of the door. Everything caught my eye, but it didn't mean that everything was good for my students. It's the same when we open our mailboxes or inboxes and are besieged by an onslaught of ads for materials—overwhelming and difficult to weed through. The expertise of the educators around us—in and beyond the school building—is a valuable tool when choosing the best for your students. Social media is a great way to reach educators around the world. Using platforms like Facebook groups, Twitter, Instagram, and Pinterest, we can find resources that other educators have tried and recommended. From there, we can carefully consider whether the tools they use are also the best tools for our students right now.

Who Wrote This Resource?

A constant question to keep in mind as you review resources is "Who wrote this?" Whether teacher created or company created, it's worth researching the author(s) to get a better idea of their reputation in the field, their motivations for providing the resource, and even their core ideas about education and children.

Using this chart to inventory our current materials and approaches gives us a clear picture of the stages, skills, groupings, and outcomes that our approaches and materials support. For example, I may find that I have too many resources that are appropriate for whole-group and not enough that address small-group instruction. This tells me that I need to prioritize small-group instruction when I'm looking for new ideas and materials. On the other hand, if I find that one cell is packed with more notes than others, I might consider: Am I overemphasizing a particular stage, skill, grouping, outcome, or Depth of Knowledge level?

Does It Help My Students Meet the Goals That Have Been Set for Them?

During my first few years as a teacher, my classroom was built as the train was moving. I remembered waiting for payday to buy the cutest, most colorful, and most cost-efficient materials to stock my classroom. In addition, toward the end of the school year, teachers would sit furniture, materials, and resources in the hallways as a courtesy for newer teachers. It was exciting! Beggars can't be choosers, right? Well, I've learned that may be true for bookcases and bins, but we all need to be choosy when it comes to books and classroom resources.

Sometimes resources are chosen based on availability and price tag. As a result, the alignment of the resource can be an afterthought. But basing choices on what's easy to find and inexpensive can be costly in the long run if the resources we choose don't help our students meet the goals we have for them.

Alignment with What *Your* Students Need

At the end of the previous chapter, you identified:

- the skills and concepts for which your students need support most urgently
- the particular student need for which you will be seeking in new resources or approaches

Keep those notes and your tracker in front of you as you consider resources, and ask yourself, "Will this resource help my students with the needs I know they have? Will this resource work with their accommodations and interests?" If not, the resource is not what you're looking for—even if it is fun, recommended, or free.

Alignment with What *Children* Need Each Day

None of us became teachers to assign a flood of worksheets or to give daily practice tests, but many of us have found ourselves spending a great deal of precious time doing these kinds of activities. I have often seen the shift of a classroom from being student centered to being teacher centered because of the perceived need to cover content prior to the high-stakes testing window.

When we consider *what* a resource proposes to do for our children, we also need to consider *how* the resource proposes to do it. Students learn more than content at school—they also learn from the ways we teach and the ways they are required to participate in their learning. If we use a resource that requires students to spend all of their reading time at school filling in worksheets or watching videos, without any opportunities to immerse themselves in books, what are we teaching them about what it means to read? At a time when we face intense pressure to achieve higher scores and dramatic improvements, it may be tempting to adopt a resource that claims to promise results, even if it means turning our backs on practices that make school joyful, engaging, and meaningful for our students. "It's just for a little while," we might think, "just until the state test is over." However, if we want students to make gains that outlast a single assessment and lead to a lifetime of learning, we can't sacrifice the kind of instruction that we know children need.

Alignment with Standards

Although we all have our own goals for our students, most of us also have a set of standards that we are required to address. When we consider approaches and materials for our classrooms, we do not need to limit what we do in the classroom to what the standards prescribe. However, we can find innovative ideas and tools that will help us to address the standards. Often, there are essential skills that live within each standard. This allows teachers to broaden their criteria for resources that address standards by providing additional practice opportunities for key skills during instruction. Anchor charts, graphic organizers, and so on become more useful because teachers are not limited to the wording of each standard and can differentiate where needed.

In the past, my district has learned the hard way that an "alignment" sticker on the cover of a resource does not mean that it adequately teaches required standards. We have seen companies quickly provide a "revised" version of a program to catch up with changes to our required standards. Because we were rushed to implement the new standards, we did not have a lot of time to validate or invalidate the companies' claims. The easier choice was to roll with the new product. We found that the program's formative assessments were not good indicators of students' performance on our annual state assessment: the program wasn't helping kids to meet the standards. In addition, it was challenging to clearly identify exactly where the gaps were within the program so that we could supplement lessons.

The following year, we realized that we couldn't solely rely on one program to meet the standards. Our school began a deep dive into each

Reinforcing Key Standards Vocabulary Across the School Day

When you look at the standards with the lens of finding nouns and verb, you can also take one more step to help with standards alignment—looking for Tier 2 words to use across the school day, in all content areas.

In their influential *Bringing Words to Life*, Beck, McKeown, and Kucan (2013) propose that there are three "tiers" of words: Tier 1 words are basic words that are in most children's vocabularies. Tier 2 words are high-frequency words used by mature language users across several content areas. Examples of Tier 2 words include *explain*, *compare*, *infer*, *cite*, *demonstrate*, *conclude*, *organize*, and *observe*. Tier 3 words are not frequently used except in specific content areas or domains. Tier 3 words are central to building knowledge and conceptual understanding within the various academic domains and are integral to instruction of content, but each Tier 3 word is specific to a particular content area. Examples of Tier 3 words include *photosynthesis*, *protest*, *figurative language*, *cubic*, *algorithm*, *editorial*, *historical*, and *idiom*.

Although it is not important for students to know tier words, it is useful for teachers to be aware of these tiers so that they can increase students' exposure to Tier 2 and Tier 3 words throughout the day. Allowing students to copy words and definitions in a workbook is not as useful as allowing students to use those same words in a cooperative group setting with discussion starter cards. When we use key Tier 2 words in language arts, science, mathematics, and social studies, we reinforce key vocabulary across the school day. In addition, if students don't fully understand Tier 3 words, then they risk not grasping key concepts or content throughout each subject area.

In my school, we used Unpacking the Standards document (Figure 2.2) to identify activities and resources in the building to help teach that standard. By doing this, we were able to consider how technology, leveled libraries, science kits, artifacts, and much more aligned with our standards. One major bonus of using this formula was that we could easily align the assessments to the practice opportunities that students experienced. It was a win-win for the teachers and students.

content area's standards. Prior to each unit, we began to unpack the actual standards. This helped us to leave the planning table with the same understandings and expectations. We used a simple formula to get to the heart of each standard: verbs + nouns = standard.

The nouns were what students were expected to "know" and the verbs were what the students were expected to "do." As you can see in Figure 2.2, teachers unpacked Common Core Reading Informational Standard 1 for fourth-grade students.

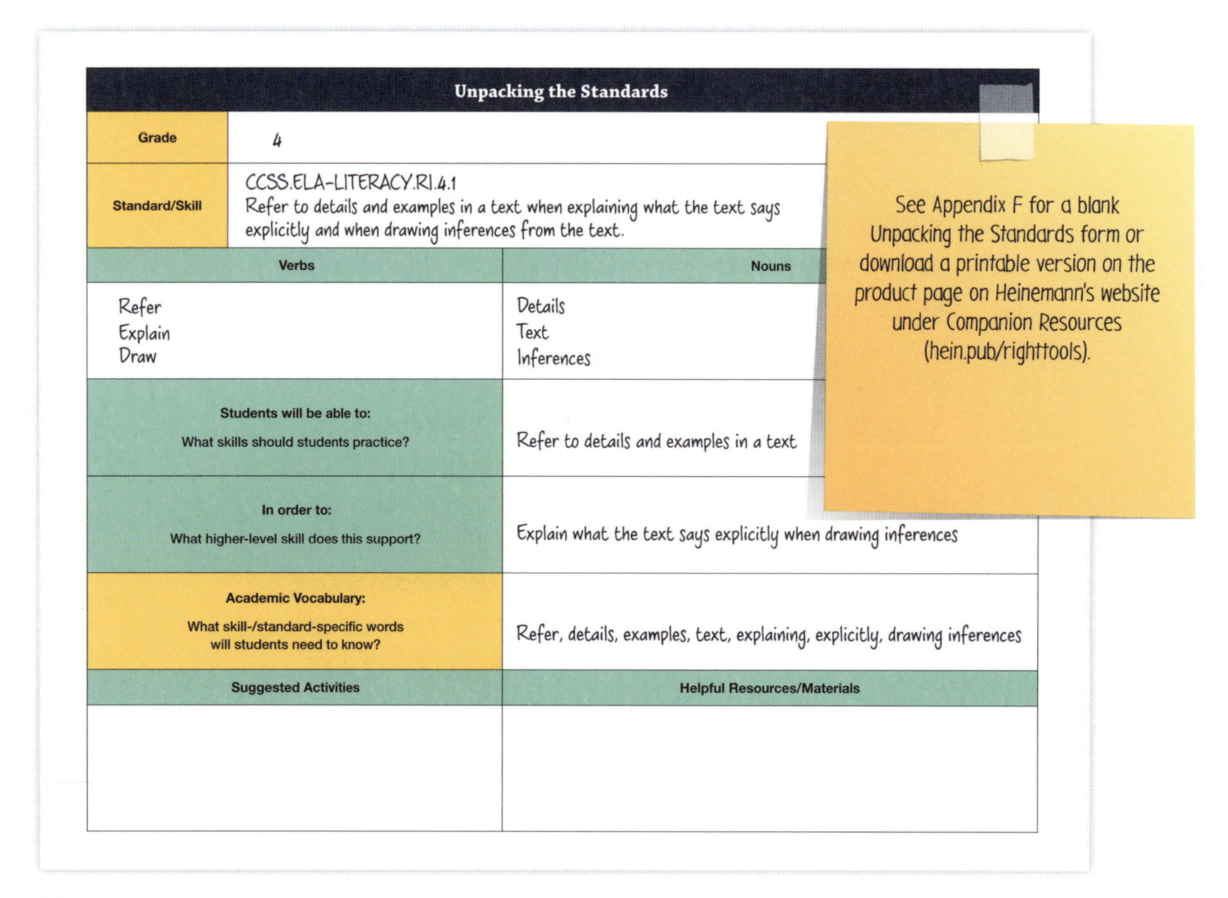

Unpacking the Standards	
Grade	4
Standard/Skill	CCSS.ELA-LITERACY.RI.4.1 Refer to details and examples in a text when explaining what the text says explicitly and when drawing inferences from the text.
Verbs	Nouns
Refer Explain Draw	Details Text Inferences
Students will be able to: What skills should students practice?	Refer to details and examples in a text
In order to: What higher-level skill does this support?	Explain what the text says explicitly when drawing inferences
Academic Vocabulary: What skill-/standard-specific words will students need to know?	Refer, details, examples, text, explaining, explicitly, drawing inferences
Suggested Activities	Helpful Resources/Materials

See Appendix F for a blank Unpacking the Standards form or download a printable version on the product page on Heinemann's website under Companion Resources (hein.pub/righttools).

Figure 2.2 An Example of Unpacking the Standards

Is There Research That Will Tell You More About It?

You may find that some resources, especially large-scale comprehensive programs (basal readers, for example) and established instructional approaches (such as the workshop model, guided reading, and balanced literacy), present themselves as research based. But what does that mean?

In 2002, the U.S. Department of Education's Institute of Education Sciences created the What Works Clearinghouse (WWC) to provide educators, policy makers, and the public with a central and trusted source of scientific evidence of what works in education. The WWC is committed to ensuring that its products and services meet user needs. The WWC uses randomized controlled trials (RCTs), and one of the distinguishing characteristics of an RCT is that study subjects are randomly assigned to one of two groups, which are differentiated by whether they receive the intervention. When you use the WWC to research a particular program, the site will offer an assessment of the program's efficacy, based on studies that meet its criteria for rigor. The WWC can also tell you the race, ethnicity, gender, socioeconomic status, and language status of the students involved in the cited studies.

Although the WWC's assessments can help you spot resources that have not proven effective, they don't guarantee if a resource will or won't be effective in your classroom. The WWC assessments cannot tell you how well a particular tool will work for each of your own students or whether the tool will help you to meet the goals that have been set for your students. As the authors of *The Handbook of Reading Research* (Kamil et al. 2011) explain, when considering a program, "an emphasis on *what* works needs to be accompanied by an analysis of *why* and *how* various practices or curricula work for which students" (xviii).

Are "Research-Based" Programs Really Research Based?

In education, the terms *scientifically based research* and *research-based* are used interchangeably, and usually without the kind of proof that the WWC requires. These terms are meant to reassure school and district leaders, who are feeling the pressure of increased accountability around student achievement. Often, these leaders rely heavily on the reputation of the vendor and do not always have time to test programs to ensure that they're the best fit for the students they serve.

Educational researcher Peter Dewitz has studied the major basal/core reading programs and interviewed authors, publishers, and editors who worked on these programs to learn about how the programs are made. Dewitz argues that core reading programs are rarely faithful to the research they claim to be aligned with, that they omit valid instructional ideas because the ideas don't align with what a publisher is selling, and that there are few trustworthy studies that prove the programs are effective. Because of this, he concludes, "the use of the label *research-based* conveys a certainty that does not exist" (Dewitz and Wolskee 2012, 11).

When a Research-Based Program Falls Short

So what happens when we use those research-based materials in our classes and the results aren't favorable? When someone says that the program works, but we find that it isn't working for our students?

When a district or school puts its faith in the program, not the teachers, the "compliance monster" begins to slowly rear its ugly head. In these cases, districts and schools equate fidelity with a false sense of effective instructional delivery, requiring teachers to read the teacher's manual page by page and never allowing teachers to determine how to differentiate instruction, but allowing the differentiation section in the manual to determine what that process looks like. As a result, I often heard teachers say, "Just tell me what you want me to say" or "What page do you want me to turn to?" Being told what to do seemed preferable to being perceived as dangerously out of compliance. The decision makers shifted from the classroom teacher to the front office building or even the district, moving the focus further away from the student.

When teachers are given research-based materials that address the masses but not the warm bodies that occupy the desks in their own classroom, their effectiveness is jeopardized. Even programs that are considered effective may not be so for every student in every situation. Harvard professor of educational leadership Richard F. Elmore puts it more directly: "The single biggest observational discipline we have to teach people in our networks is to look on top of the desk, rather than at the teacher in front of the room" (2008). The light bulb comes on when educators understand that *research-based* means that a program *can* work, but that we may need to adjust it to address the unique needs of each student on our roster. Students' behaviors determine how a resource can be maximized in the learning process.

So in a nutshell, a research-based label cannot be our sole determining factor in deciding what materials to use with our students. We must empower ourselves so that companies cannot present prepackaged materials with an alignment sticker affixed to the top and force our hand in adopting the resource.

Questions to Consider When Examining Research-Based Materials

The following questions can help us to consider whether a resource will be a good fit for our students.

- When was research conducted?
    - Education is ever evolving and so are resources. As an educator, it's important to know the era in which the resource was validated. Even though we may believe that they are tried and true, resources used during our childhood can be outdated. We need to ensure that our resources engage the new fast-paced highly stimulated learner.

- What were the demographics of the participants?
    - There is a myth out there that says that educational resources should follow a one-size-fits-all approach. If so, it would save us all a lot of time and money! Unfortunately, that is not the case and students need resources that can be easily adjusted to improve individual performance. Considering variables such as gender, race, and age can help us to predict whether something will be successful with the students we teach. For example, resources used in schools with a large English Language Learners population will look different than in a school with a large special education population. Of course, we can't capture our students' unique characteristics with these wide categories. As the National

Education Association (NEA) reminds us, there are a myriad of factors that affect students and their needs in the classroom. Keep the individuals in your room in mind as you consider resources.

- What was the instructional delivery method used to gather data for the study?
  - The instructional delivery method is the way in which teachers engage students during the lesson. This could be in whole group, in small group, or one on one. Knowing how the resource was used with participants will give us an idea of how we'll likely want to use the resource with our own students. And, if we're looking for help with whole-group instruction, for example, we'll keep that requirement in mind as we consider options.

Putting It into Practice

Determining whether a resource is "good" or not requires us to look at a variety of data, to scrutinize resources, to consider a host of factors, and to assess and track student progress. Let's take a moment now to remind ourselves of why we're doing this work.

During my time as an instructional coach, I had the opportunity to work with primary-grades teachers. I distinctly remember one kindergartener, Diega, a quiet girl who came to school speaking little English. Our baseline reading assessments ranked Diega at "high risk" for not achieving end-of-year goals. For two semesters, her teacher, Ms. Jones, worked with Diega four days a week for twenty minutes on targeted skills. Ms. Jones monitored Diega's progress weekly and used her findings to determine next steps in instruction. She drew from a variety of materials and approaches: alphabet arcs that helped with phonemic awareness and phonics, timed fluency passages, guiding comprehension questions during partner reading, teacher think-alouds with questioning that was mindful

of Depth of Knowledge levels, and scheduled formative assessments that were aligned with daily instruction.

Diega's performance and motivation began to shift, and each administration of the summative assessment showed improvement. By the end of the year, Diega had gained a whole year of progress. Her end-of-year assessment proclaimed her at "low risk" for not achieving end-of-year goals. More importantly, she was *reading* and was a more confident student. It was inspiring for both the student and the teacher!

Ms. Jones could simply have worked through a single program, or she might have stuck with lesson plans she'd used before and been comfortable with, but she knew that wasn't what Diega needed. Being consistent and intentional had a direct correlation to Diega's overall growth. Meeting a student's needs through careful consideration of the factors mentioned in this chapter can improve the most important part of our schools . . . our students.

Conversation Starters

Colleagues, instructional coaches, and administrators can be valuable resources for ideas and feedback as you consider what you'll look for in resources and approaches. A few questions might lead to helpful discussions:

- What tools would you recommend for determining if a resource is helpful for students?
- When determining the reliability of a resource, how do you suggest ensuring that it meets the needs of my students?
- What educational search tools have been vetted by other teachers within my school?
- What are some options for assessing the alignment of resources to provide meaningful skills or standards-driven learning opportunities?

Chapter 3

How Will I Use It?

I remember my first-year teacher mentor, Ms. Haines. Her class had been identified as the bottom 20 percent of the entire grade level. The school had given her a yearlong systematic intervention program, a one-stop shop that had proven results in other states and even around the world. However, it didn't seem to be working for her students. So, Ms. Haines took a different approach: Instead of basing her instruction on what the program dictated, she began basing her instruction on what her students needed. She lugged her teacher manuals home every evening and combed through the resources and activities in the program, looking for tools and ideas to help the specific children in her classroom, using what she needed when she needed it, not following the program page by page. This work required her to know her students well, to make her own decisions, and to design her instruction to meet her students' needs. And it paid off. By the end of this accelerated program, students made remarkable gains in their performance in reading, and many of them transitioned to a general education classroom the following year. Some went from needing a full day of intervention support to only a daily forty-five-minute block of support.

I admired Ms. Haines' approach, but I was hesitant to try it myself. When I first began teaching, I did not know where to begin. For fear of making a mistake, I began my planning by flipping to the directions page rather than by considering what my students needed. I figured the experts were the people who created the resource, not realizing that I was the expert on my own students. At the time, this felt like the safe route. Unfortunately, the safe route was not the route my students needed. The result was that my students were constantly dependent on me. When faced with assessments—situations when I was not there to support them—they couldn't do the work.

I wish I could say that my story is unique, but it's not. I know many teachers who feel that they must follow instructions or approaches faithfully, even when things don't seem to be working and students aren't making the gains we'd like. We find ways to blame ourselves or, worse, our students, for a lack of success, instead of reconsidering the tools themselves. Additionally, educational companies know how to market and capture the attention of educators quickly. The pressures and time demands of our jobs make it tempting to teach from an all-inclusive box.

This is not to say that we should reinvent the wheel in our classrooms: There is much to be learned from strong resources and from teaching approaches that others have pioneered and refined. However, as we begin to use a new tool or a new approach, our role is not simply to implement it without considering our students. Our job is to be like Ms. Haines: to determine how we will use resources and approaches based on what *our students* need. Using a resource for the sake of using it is not enough to move the needle. We have to be intentional.

In the previous chapters, you've identified your students' strengths and needs as well as the goals you want them to achieve, and you've looked at potential resources and approaches carefully with these specifics in mind. In this chapter, we'll consider how to use these new ideas and tools in ways that are targeted to address particular goals, appropriate and engaging for your students, and scaffolded to promote student mastery and independence.

Keep Your Focus Clear

So often I see an instructional focus being determined based on the resource that a teacher has and not by the data before them. Letting your resources decide the focus for your instruction can be, at best, a waste of both your time and your student's time. At worst, it can undermine students' success and motivation. There is nothing more frustrating for students and teachers alike than engaging in an activity that is not purposeful or well tailored to students.

Look back on the notes on your tracker: What is your focus?

Begin with this end in mind, before you even begin to consider how to implement the new idea or tool you have in mind. Consider: *What, specifically, do you want students to be able to do as a result of this work?* When you consider this question with your students in mind, you may find that you have different goals for different students. It's OK to name several goals if you need to. After all, each child in your class has his or her own strengths and needs.

Decide What to Use in the Resource or Approach

When we identify a purpose for our work with our students, it becomes easier to look at resources and approaches critically. Instead of reading through the teacher's manuals and instructions with the aim of simply complying with them, we can read them with an eye toward whether/how they match our specific goals for our students.

As an instructional coach, I supported teachers with planning and executing lessons. I observed a teacher during her literacy block. She was teaching her second graders homophones because there were lessons, activities, and worksheets located within the provided basal reader series. Unfortunately, they did not meet any of the required grade-level standards, and her students had much more pressing needs in their literacy instruction: The majority of her students struggled with reading on-level text. The resource that she was using may have proved useful later in the year, when the children were reading with greater proficiency, but it was not appropriate for that time.

Teaching resources may be eager to prescribe an order, a timeline, or a structure for you to adhere to in your teaching. However, you, not the resource, know your students best. It is essential that we prioritize our lessons based on our students' needs and not allow the resource to determine the focus. As you look at what a resource offers, zero in on the focus you've named for your students: How will this resource help with that focus? What aspects of this resource will you use for that focus? What aspects can you set aside for now? Use what your students need when they need it.

Begin Your Plan: With Whom Will You Use This Resource or Approach, and How?

Now that you've considered both what you want for your students and what the resource or approach can provide, it's time to consider who you will use it with and how you'll introduce it. No matter how a resource or approach presents itself, it's up to you to decide how to use it in your classroom.

The first question to consider is how you'll group students for this work. See Figure 3.1 for options for student groupings.

Using the Resource or Approach with Whole-Group Instruction

As teachers, we know both the benefits and drawbacks of whole-group instruction. On one hand, we can address every student at once. On the

Options for Student Groupings

If . . .	Try . . .
• You have the same goal in mind for all or very nearly all of your students *or* • You're introducing a new skill *or* • The instruction is on a level that is easily accessible to all or very nearly all of your students	Using the new resource or approach with the **whole class**
• You have different goals for different groups of students *or* • The instruction is on a level that will be challenging to students *or* • Groups of students need varying levels of support with a skill *or* • The instruction offers targeted remediation	Using the new resource or approach with **small groups**
• You have very targeted goals for a few students *or* • You have a student who needs more challenge than the other students *or* • You have a student who needs more support than the other students	Using the new resource or approach with **one-on-one** or **individualized instruction**

Figure 3.1 Options for Student Groupings

other, we know that whole-class instruction can also be a time when we lose students' attention, energy, and motivation.

That said, if you find that your entire class will benefit from the new tool or approach you're about to implement, you can design your whole-class instruction to be as effective as possible by moving away for the "sit and get" model. Yes, the quickest way to disseminate information is to dish it out, but the quickest way to learning is to gradually release the responsibility from teacher to student. You'll see further explanation of the gradual release of responsibility model later in the chapter.

Using the Resource or Approach with Small-Group Instruction

Magic can happen in small groups. I still smile when I think of the "happy dance" I saw teachers do at one school when they saw the gains their students were making as a result of just thirty minutes a day of small-group instruction in reading. They'd used formative assessments to form groups. Then, they'd created center activities targeted to their goals for students, which gave them additional opportunities for practice during instruction: fluency phones to improve fluency intonation and tone, sorting cards that allowed students to increase their vocabulary using word association groups, and Venn diagrams that helped students compare and contrast concepts within text. As they were able to better see each child's successes and needs, they were better able to identify resources that would assist them in supporting their students. Each week, teachers gave students practice opportunities and closely monitored their movement while working with them in a teacher-led group.

This might sound like a lot of moving parts. The keys are keeping your focus on the kids in front of you and having a clear purpose in mind for each group. Once you have those, everything else falls in line. Here are some quick planning tips for preparing for group work in your class. You can also use the Grouping Planner (Figure 3.3 on p. 54) as a tool to get started with the planning process.

Form Groups

Look back on your tracker to consider what you know about your students. If you can identify clusters of students for whom you have similar goals, you might make those clusters your groups. If you can see groups of students who will master a skill more or less quickly than others, you might use this distinction to form groups. If you are aiming to help your students work more collaboratively and to draw from each other's strengths, consider academically heterogeneous groupings—groupings that include students with a range of skill levels. Academically heterogeneous grouping allows for groups based on interests, learning preferences, and experiences. If you've formed a group based on a trait that each student can take pride in, consider letting students know up front how groups were chosen. This can foster intrinsic motivation and a sense of ownership.

Another option is to give students the options to choose their own groups. The freedom to choose their own groups can be a powerful motivator for students and can help them to feel that they have a voice in their own learning.

Groups don't need to be permanent. Flexible groupings—in which we continuously change groups based on the assigned activity or purpose—promote collaboration and give students opportunities to engage in academic conversations that include divergent perspectives.

Groups are more effective when student-to-teacher ratios are minimal and there is a clear focus. When planning for groups, aim for about four to six groups in one class period, with at least two and no more than six students in a group.

Plan Your Group Work Time

To make group work part of your daily plan, schedule weekly rotations to ensure that you are working with each group on a regular basis. Figure 3.2 is an example of weekly teacher small-group rotation, with each rotation lasting 15–20 minutes. In the rotation are four different groups of students:

- **Beginner:** performing two or more grade levels below
- **Developing:** performing below grade level
- **Proficient:** performing on grade level
- **Distinguished:** performing above grade level

In the rotation, the amount of support is tiered. Students with the most need are more frequently seen by the teacher and require explicit and systematic instruction.

The Grouping Planner in Figure 3.3 (on p. 54) can be a helpful tool in considering options for forming and scheduling groups.

Maximize Your Group Work

Entire books have been written on teaching in small groups, and for good reason: Small groups dramatically decrease the student-to-teacher ratio, can provide more targeted instruction than whole-class instruction, and

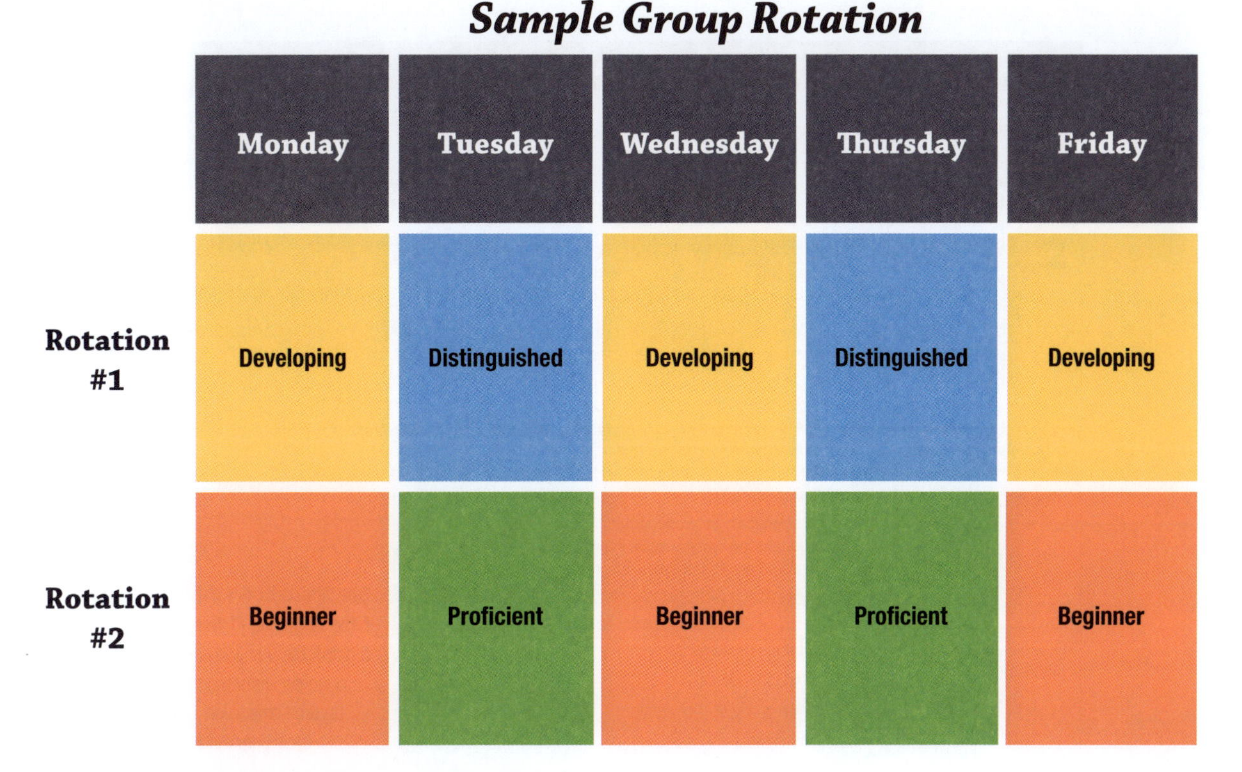

Figure 3.2 Sample Group Rotation

can be more manageable and sustainable than individual instruction. Here are a few guiding principles to keep in mind as you get started:

- ***Use the pieces of the resource that address the focus you have set for the group.*** For example, if you're working with a group that needs more practice with consonant blends, start with the resource's lessons on that topic. You don't need to begin using the resource's initial lessons on individual consonants, such as /t/ or /n/, just because that's the order the resource uses. Give your students what they need right now.
- ***Don't use the resource with a group that doesn't need it.*** There's no need to use a resource across all groups if it doesn't serve a purpose for every group.

Grouping Planner		
Academic Purpose/Goal:		
Decisions to Be Made	**Options**	**How This Plan Benefits Your Students**
Who will choose the groups?	☐ Teacher ☐ Students	
If the groups are teacher chosen, how will they be determined?	☐ Academically homogeneous (grouped by goal or by readiness/ skill level) ☐ Academically heterogeneous (grouped by learning style, interest, or some other characteristic)	
How big will the groups be?	☐ Partners (2 students) ☐ Triad (3 students) ☐ Small group (4–5 students) ☐ Split class	
How will the groups use class time?	• Frequency of meetings: ☐ Single meeting ☐ Multiple meetings over a few days ☐ Multiple meetings for more than a week • Length of each meeting: ☐ Less than one class period ☐ One class period	
How will the groups be flexible?	☐ Whole class ☐ Small group ☐ Partner	

See Appendix G for a larger copy of the Grouping Planner or download a printable version on the product page on Heinemann's website under Companion Resources (hein.pub/righttools).

Figure 3.3 Grouping Planner

- ***Make every minute count.*** To keep focused on the day's lesson, establish consistent group routines from the onset. Students should be familiar with transitions between rotations, setup and cleanup, and expectations within the group. Providing students with explicit and systematic instruction on an identified skill can assist with maximizing each moment.
- ***Make specific plans for each group.*** Small groups give you the power to target students' needs and strengths more specifically than whole-class instruction does. If you find yourself teaching exactly the same lesson in exactly the same way with multiple groups, you're not taking advantage of this opportunity. Figure 3.4 shows how a teacher might differentiate instruction for three different groups on the same skill: asking and answering questions. Note that although some of the resources are used across groups, they are used differently to meet each group's specific goals.

A Sample Plan for Group Work Differentiation

Goal: *Formulate questions and answers that demonstrate their understanding of the text and cite specific examples.*

	Group 1: Remediate	Group 2: Teach	Group 3: Accelerate
Description of group	In this group, students may struggle with foundational skills needed to master the grade-level objective or goal.	In this group, students already have the foundational skills needed to master the grade-level objective or goal.	In this group, students have mastered the grade-level objective or goal.
Resources	Detail cards (each card names a key detail from the text) Leveled text (below-level)	5Ws (Who, What, When, Where, Why, and How) graphic organizer Leveled text (on level)	Writing journal Leveled text (above level)
Other materials	Sticky notes	Highlighters	Index cards Highlighters
Activity	Cards with key details from the leveled text will be distributed to students. After reading the text, students will sort the cards into two piles: details that they could recall from the text and details that they did not recognize after reading the text. Students then revisit the text and create a question for each unfamiliar key detail.	After reading the text, students will identify questions and add them to the 5Ws graphic organizer. After switching graphic organizers with a partner, they will use the highlighter to locate the answers in the text.	Students will read the text and write questions about key details in the margins of the text. Next, index cards with text-dependent questions will be distributed to students. Students will reread the text and highlight the key detail that answers the question. The students will construct a response to their question that includes key details that were highlighted within the text.

Figure 3.4 A Sample Plan for Group Work Differentiation

- ***Recognize differences within groups.*** Even within a homogeneous grouping, all children bring their own strengths and needs. Consider how you will tailor the work to each child within the group. For example, you might use the seating arrangement for the group to help support the students who need you the most—which seats give those students the best eye contact with you?
- ***Give heterogeneous groups a clear structure.*** Giving students in heterogeneous groups roles—such as timekeeper, recorder, reporter, troubleshooter, or coordinator—can help all the students in a heterogeneous grouping feel that they have a voice in the learning process.

Using the Resource or Approach with One-on-One or Individualized Instruction

Sometimes, even a well-run small group doesn't meet all of a student's needs. When I was a third-grade teacher, I had a student named Jaylen. He was a little boy who loved to learn. He grasped concepts so quickly

that it became a challenge to keep up with him. I found myself struggling to find productive things for him to do after he finished his work. Sadly, as a new teacher, I found that my college degree had equipped me to teach to the masses but not to individuals. I began pulling materials and finding new challenges for Jaylen that extended the learning and built upon what was mastered that day: projects, presentations, and more.

Although some individualized instruction might involve one-on-one time with a teacher, one-on-one time is not always necessary. The individualized instruction Jaylen received, for example, didn't always need to involve me: Often, he worked with materials on his own. The determining factor here is not whether the instruction is delivered one-to-one, but that it's tailored to the student and that it proceeds at the student's pace.

Refine Your Plan: How Will You Move Students Toward Independence?

Our goal for all of our students is that they will use the skills we teach them independently. So, when we're piloting a resource, we need to plan for that same outcome, even if the resource itself isn't structured to do this. As you're planning across a unit or a term, build in opportunities to gradually release the responsibility to students by modeling and continuously checking for understanding. When we gradually shift "all the responsibility for performing a task . . . to a situation in which the students assume all of the responsibility," students grow (Duke and Pearson 2002, 210–11). Figure 3.5 outlines the teacher's behaviors versus the student's behaviors throughout this process.

All these phases are fluid and may not be completed in one class period. Some skills, activities, or tasks may require longer times in each phase, and, at times, you may find yourself needing to go back to the "I do" or "we do" stages to clarify before moving back to the "you do" stages. As always, our work should focus on where our students are and what they need in the moment. Overall, however, as Figure 3.6 shows, the path for each skill should be that teacher responsibility decreases while student responsibility increases.

Teacher and Student Behaviors in Gradual Release of Responsibility

Component	Teacher Behavior	Student Behavior
Focus lesson "I do"	• Provides direct instruction • Establishes goals and purpose • Models • Thinks aloud	• Actively listens • Asks for clarification
Guided instruction "We do"	• Provides interactive instruction • Works with students • Gives whole-group instruction • Uses students' mistakes to formatively assess	• Asks and responds to questions • Works with teacher and classmates • Student leads • Opportunities for student modeling • Allowed to make mistakes
Productive group work (collaborative) "You do it together"	• Uses student talk as a formative assessment to provide feedback and determine next steps • Clarifies confusion	• Works in small groups • Works with classmates, shares outcomes • Collaborates on same task with new example/problem • Looks to peers for clarification
Independent learning "You do it alone"	• Evaluates • Determines level of understanding • Does not assist student	• Works alone • Demonstrates individual understanding of the process/content with a new example • Takes full responsibility for outcome

Figure 3.5 Teacher and Student Behaviors in Gradual Release of Responsibility

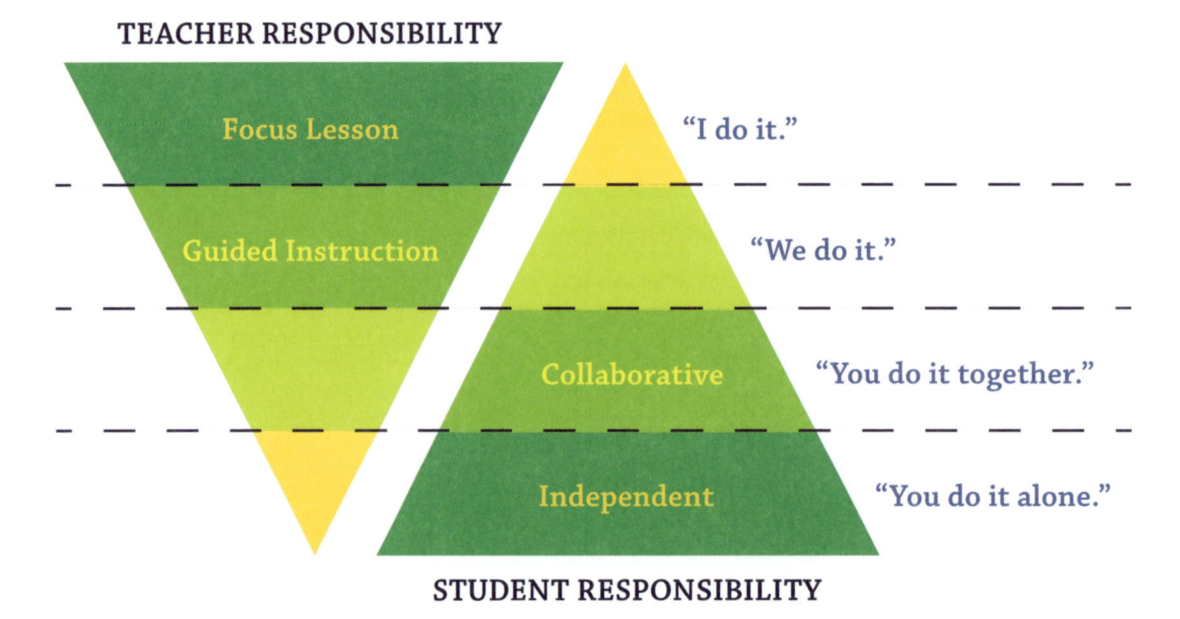

Figure 3.6 The Gradual Release of Responsibility

You may find that the resource or approach you're piloting does not take this gradual release of responsibility into account. It may offer lessons that keep you firmly at the center of instruction. Its tools may not give students the opportunities to apply skills on their own. For example, a graphic organizer designed to support students' ability to identify the main idea and key details in a particular passage might have three numbered bubbles, giving students a clue that there are three key details in the passage. These tools can be helpful in the focus lesson, the guided instruction, and perhaps even the collaborative work. However, these structures don't give students the opportunity to practice the skill independently, which is the final stage of the gradual release of responsibility. If the resource you're using doesn't give students this option, you will need to consider how to build in opportunities for students to show their independent mastery of a skill. Using the example of the graphic organizer, you might use the premade graphic organizer for the focus lesson and guided instruction. But, when it's time to ask students to use the skill independently, give them a blank page to organize their ideas, asking them to create a graphic organizer based on what makes sense for the text at hand.

Putting It into Practice

No matter what a resource or approach may promise us, our focus—and our responsibility—is with our students. It might feel easier or safer to follow a resource's step-by-step instructions, starting on page 1, but our jobs aren't about following directions. They're about meeting our students where they are and helping them move forward.

When I taught third grade, I had a student named Alyssa. She loved to learn but, at the beginning of the year, she barely spoke and often sat by herself at lunch. Because she spoke to others so little, it was challenging to see where she was academically. If I'd simply stuck with the basal I was using at the time, marching through the lessons using the pacing guide that the program provided, I doubt that I'd ever have heard Alyssa

Conversation Starters

Colleagues, instructional coaches, and administrators can be valuable resources for ideas and feedback as you plan how you'll use new resources and approaches. A few questions might lead to helpful discussions:

- Have you used this resource or approach? If so, what was helpful about it? What advice would you give about using it?
- How could we use our professional learning communities or planning meetings to discuss how we can use resources strategically?
- I'm looking into new ways to structure my instructional time. What structures have worked for you? How have they been helpful?
- I'm trying to differentiate instruction using a variety of resources in small groups. What kinds of resources do you use in your small-group instruction? Is there anything you'd recommend I try?

speak or seen her grow academically. Instead, I observed her interactions with classmates she felt comfortable with and began grouping them by interests and not by ability. The students began to naturally work collaboratively. At each meeting, they used role cards I'd given them to determine who would do what. I noticed that her role changed throughout the year. First she was the "Go-fer" and gathered all of the materials, then she became the "Recorder" and wrote down the groups ideas. By the end of the year, Alyssa was the "Reporter" and shared with the class the group's thoughts: a major accomplishment for her. Because she was provided with a safe environment for taking risks, her confidence grew and her academic progress began to follow. Many other aspects of the basal were still useful to us, but my students needed something other than the lockstep pacing the program suggested.

Resources and approaches may have gold inside, but when we follow them without taking into account what our students need, we lose focus, and our students' success suffers. When we use resources strategically, we can unlock the magic within them.

Is It Working for My Students?

All of us have something that we love to use in the classroom. Early in my teaching career, I got excited when I could read books about the beach to my students. It was my most favorite place to be, and I lit up when I could reminisce on any aspect of this topic. I paused on each page and shared personal stories about my experiences. This might have been a fun experience for me, but it wasn't a very useful strategy when I was

trying to teach main idea and how to find key details to my third graders. Thankfully, I had a good mentor teacher and a system of formative assessments in place and, when my students did *not* blow that formative assessment out of the water, I could tell right away that my beach books and my approach were not giving my students what they needed. I needed to make a change, and fast.

Being the best for your students means that we are constantly reflecting on what is working and what is not working within our classrooms. In this chapter, we'll assess whether the resources and approaches we're using are working and consider what our next steps should be.

How Do I Know If I Am on Track?

When we're doing the day-to-day work of teaching, it can be hard to focus on the bigger picture and not to get caught up in each day's details. We often know what we want our students to be able to do, but in order to do what? Getting another perspective, via a mentor, a coach, or an assessment, can prevent us from spending entire lessons focusing on things that don't relate to the "in order to" part of an objective.

Use Frequent Checkpoint Assessments to Monitor Progress

Using formative assessment at specific points within the grade-level curriculum, or checkpoints, helps us to gauge students' performance on a standardized, grade-level performance scale for each particular skill or standard. Although these checkpoints may be determined by the school's curriculum and/or scope and sequence (perhaps midsemester or midunit), we can also set them ourselves, as necessary. For example, when I was in the classroom, I monitored students' progress weekly.

Each checkpoint identifies the skills or standards against which we can assess students' progress. For example, second-grade students may be expected to compare the main topic and key details between two pieces of informational text. Therefore, at a checkpoint, we may choose to determine if a student understands how to identify the main topic and key details in one text before asking the child to compare the main topic and key details of two pieces of text.

Once we have results from these checkpoints and we've compared these results to the baseline data we collected on the Student Progress Tracker (see p. 3 in Chapter 1), we can trace the rate of student improvement back to the instruction the student has received. We can use this process to evaluate individual progress or the progress of an entire class. This helps us to see whether the work we've been doing with students and the tools we've been relying on are working or whether we need to adjust our course.

To be clear, progress monitoring should not only occur with our developing-level students; it is also necessary for our proficient and exemplary-level students. So often, we use resources as a tool to identify the needs of lower-performing students but fail to reinforce and accelerate for the other students in the classroom. We want all of our students to leave our classes stronger than when they entered them.

Reflect on Your Students' Progress with a Mentor or a Coach

During my first year of teaching, my school assigned me a mentor, and we met to reflect on the "glows and grows" in my classroom each week. This process required me to rethink my work in the classroom. Some reflective questions that we discussed each week were:

- What was your instructional focus for the week?
- In what areas have you seen success in your instructional practice for the week?
- Did students have any lagging prerequisite skills that prohibited them from understanding the focus area for the week?
- What were your biggest challenges and what strategies did you use to overcome them?
- Are there any professional development opportunities that can help to improve your focus areas for the week?

Each question challenged the way that I planned for the upcoming week. Really thinking about what worked and what didn't was helpful because it forced me reconsider the use of my resources and best practices and to identify additional supports needed to improve student performance throughout each lesson.

The preceding questions might be helpful for you to consider on your own. Or, if you have the good fortune to have a strong mentor teacher or instructional coach, they may be able to help you to identify your class' glows and grows not only from the data you've collected, but also from classroom visits and individual conversations with you.

What Do I Do with the Results I Find? Plan Next Steps

Is your feedback telling you that resources and approaches you're using are resulting in growth for your students, or are you not seeing the results you were aiming for? As always, our end goal is to move students from being teacher dependent to being independent, not simply to have students complete assignments. To move students to independence, we must provide both opportunities to practice and immediate feedback that will help to improve their overall performance. It's similar to a patient going to the doctor and being prescribed a few days of a dosage of a prescription to determine if it needs adjustment or if it is effective. The prescription might help the patient in the long run, but it is crucial that he or she is responsive to the medication. The key word is *responsive*: if we do not use strategies and resources that students are responsive to, we could hit a brick wall. The results help us make informed decisions for next steps.

When I was in the classroom, I monitored students' progress weekly, comparing their progress to the standard (Figure 4.1). To help myself see their progression more clearly, I divided the standard itself into three levels: developing, proficient, and exemplary. In this way, I could see growth in students' skills even if they had not yet mastered the standard. To find skills within the *developing* category, I unpacked the

Common Core Standard		
CCSS.ELA-LITERACY.R1/RL.2.1: Ask and answer such questions as who, what, where, when, why, and how to demonstrate understanding of key details in a text.		
Skill: *Asking and Answering Questions*		
Developing	**Proficient**	**Exemplary**
Formulate questions and answers using key details in the text	Formulate questions and answers that include *who*, *what*, *where*, *when*, *why*, and *how* to demonstrate their understanding of the text	Formulate questions and answers that refer explicitly to the text

Figure 4.1 Looking at Stages in a Standard

previous year's standard to determine which skills needed to be in place to show proficiency. To determine what was *exemplary*, I looked at the upcoming grade to find out what proficient skills would allow students to continue to progress. Another approach is to use the standard or skill itself as the *proficient* descriptor, the skills that students need to have in place before they can master the standard or skill as the *developing* descriptor, and a somewhat more autonomous version of the standard or skill as the *exemplary* descriptor.

The results of these assessments helped me to group my students and prepare for remediation, reinforcement, or acceleration. For each group, I chose an appropriate resource that provided additional practice.

It's this comparison between where the students were and where they are that reminds us of the importance of gathering baseline data before launching into instruction. It's tempting to skip directly into action if we think we already know how to solve the problem. However, assuming that we already know what will work with our students isn't the same as making an informed decision about the next instructional step. Establishing a clear plan of action based on what you know

students need allows you to identify resources and best practices that will be used with individual students to meet their individual needs in any grade level or content area.

Adjust with the Whole Class: Press *Reset*

If you observe a common theme of misconceptions or mistakes across the class, your instruction should be for the whole class. Pressing reset is simply re-modeling your expectations for your students after the initial introduction to a skill or standard and providing students more opportunities for practice. Note that re-modeling and providing more opportunities for practice do not mean repeating the lessons that weren't successful the first time. Consider: What do students need to make the lesson work? A fresh, more high-interest text? More support? More time to practice?

Adjusting with Specific Students: Maximizing Small-Group Instruction

If you are noticing that only some of your students need additional support on a particular skill or standard, use small-group work to provide that support. Placing students into smaller groups that are based on specific needs gives us the opportunity to provide students with the most appropriate resources and use the best strategies to increase their progress. Not only is a whole reset not needed, it's counterproductive: the students who have already mastered the skill or standard are ready to move on. Revisiting what they already know will hold them back.

In Chapter 3, we talk about the phases of gradual release and how it's OK for students to move through each phase at different paces. Unfortunately, I have seen classrooms in which the transition from teacher dependence to student independence is nothing more than a checklist. There is great danger in moving the whole class through these phases at the same time if all the students are not ready. Oftentimes, students do not process new learning at the same time, because each student is unique. Students come to the table with varied strengths and weaknesses.

The first step in effective small-group work is determining the area of need: what is the assessment telling you? For example, I recall when a third-grade teacher I was coaching noticed some fluency issues with Demetrius, one of his students. We analyzed his miscues and realized that a majority of them were sight words. Upon further investigation, the teacher realized that there were a few students with that same issue, so he gave them a sight word inventory to check our hunch that sight words were the main issue. When the assessment confirmed that this was indeed the case, the teacher pulled the students into a small group to build up their sight word count. In addition, during literacy centers the teacher allowed that group to engage in sight word relays, flashcard activities, and more. Demetrius' fluency began to improve because his sight word inventory began to improve. The teacher was able to connect the dots and improve his overall reading performance.

When students experience new learning and struggle with mastery of the focus standard, it's important that the teacher has a bank of resources to get them on track. A common misconception about reteaching or remediation is that when students struggle with a task in a whole group, we can simply place them in a smaller group with the same activity and

watch them soar! Right? But if that approach didn't work before, why will it work now? Additionally, students may begin to memorize the task, which limits their practice opportunities. Here are some scaffolding strategies to try in small groups:

- ***Model with Think-Alouds.*** It's helpful for students to see the thought process that an expert (you!) goes through. Showing students how to be metacognitive—aware of how they think—helps them to see how to approach a challenge. When I first modeled my thinking for my students, I had to get into a zone, fighting the temptation to tell rather than show, but it was worth it: thinking aloud each step of the way gave students a window into my mind and a model for them to refer to as they tried the work independently.
- ***Use Students' Prior Knowledge.*** Students bring their own bank of prior knowledge to school each day. Connecting that knowledge to the work you're doing in the classroom will help to make the work more meaningful and manageable for students. For example, if vocabulary is a barrier for some of your students, use photographs to help them connect to the content.
- ***Address Vocabulary.*** Work on a specific skill can get derailed by unfamiliar vocabulary. To set students up for success with their new skill, you might pull out and preteach challenging words, connecting them to students' background knowledge whenever possible. Or, you might use a read-aloud to introduce the words, giving the students an opportunity to hear the words in context, with only a brief definition along the way.
- ***Include Visual Aids.*** In addition to making word walls, allowing students to create a visual representation or use a graphic organizer helps them deepen their understanding of the concepts being shared. Visual aids support them at their individual ability level while maintaining grade-level expectations. They are especially helpful for students who are reading below level. If you choose to use these kinds of scaffolds to support students in the moment, also consider how you will plan to move students past these supports as their skills progress. You might

begin by giving them a graphic organizer structure, gradually move them toward devising their own formats for organizing their thinking.

- ***Lengthen Wait Time.*** At times, it can feel so much easier to give students the answer to a difficult question than to wait just a few seconds more while they construct their response. However, it's worth the energy. Extending your wait time—the time between when you ask the question and when you ask a student to answer it—allows students to engage in productive struggle. Seeing the wheels turning in a student's head when you ask a question also helps to inform your next steps as a teacher.
- ***Let Students Talk It Out.*** Sometimes a quiet classroom is not a learning classroom. A turn-and-talk, a triad, or a think-pair-share allows students to truly engage during each learning task. Regardless of their age, when students participate in structured discussions, critical thinking is being fostered. Giving students opportunities to have academic discourse is a meaningful skill that will help to improve their critical thinking skills and help them to justify their stance on a topic. Providing students with resources such as question stems, conversation starter cards, or guiding questions can help spark productive conversations. Using these tools, students will stay on track with the objective or purpose of their conversations. In addition, focused conversations can support and strengthen academic vocabulary.

Add to Your Toolbox: Learn About More Resources, Approaches, and Best Practices

Among your teammates, with the instructional coach, or within your district, always ask yourself how your learning can connect to the needs of your students. Many districts provide a variety of professional learning opportunities for teachers, but without a clear understanding of how that learning addresses the issues that you are having with your students, these opportunites can be overwhelming. Being self-reflective helps us identify the areas in which we can be more effective for our students. Revisiting the student's strengths and needs that you began to identify in Chapter 1 will help you to stay focused on what is most valuable to your students.

A Word About RTI

If you are working with the Response to Intervention (RTI) framework, you are likely already familiar with a cycle of assessment and response, and the checkpoints and progress monitoring discussed in this chapter can be additional data points that you can use to monitor students' performance throughout the RTI process.

If the RTI framework is new to you, it is worth investigating further. RTI provides academic and/or behavioral intervention using a systematic and targeted plan that helps to monitor students' growth over a set amount of time. The teacher is very intentional about monitoring progress with explicit instruction that has been provided. The goal is to prevent academic failure and to respond immediately to the needs of students who benefit from additional support.

Putting It into Practice

Checkpoint assessments and gathering feedback from coaches can sound clinical and removed from children until we put a face on it. For me, a particular story from my own career is the context that reminds me of the importance of these tools.

One year, when I was in the classroom, our schoolwide performance flatlined and in some cases declined. All of us were working hard. Many of the teachers were using the same concept-based units they'd used for years—units that we had piloted and refined together and that integrated the content areas. What happened?

Our state had transitioned to new standards, which assessed different skills and concepts. Yet, some teachers had not transitioned to new units and methods. As a result, students weren't adequately prepared for the expectations that would meet them the next year. Although the end-of-year assessment eventually brought the problem to light, it could have been avoided if the classrooms had been using checkpoint assessments and if the teachers involved had reached out for feedback from the instructional coach who planned and suggested strategies to improve instruction within the classroom.

Putting a known resource or approach aside can be hard. Trying something new can take up precious time, and there's no guarantee it will work—especially not the first time we try it. Yet, if we want to ensure that we're helping students to succeed, we need to make those changes when necessary.

Additionally, as educators we often pride ourselves on knowing what our students need from us. Yet even the most experienced and intuitive educators can benefit from getting assessment data and feedback from an outside source.

Luckily, we don't have to be tied to what we've done in the past. With a clear idea of who our students are and what students need, we can keep working to help students reach their full potential.

Conversation Starters

Colleagues, instructional coaches, and administrators can be valuable resources for ideas and feedback as you plan how you'll use new resources and approaches. A few questions might lead to helpful discussions:

- What are some indicators that could help to determine if a resource is improving a student's performance?
- While differentiating instruction, how can we ensure that the skills taught support the overall grade-level expectations?
- How can we leverage quantitative and qualitative information to determine a student's response to intervention?
- How can I, as a teacher, use students' whole-group performance to inform next steps during small-group instruction?

Chapter 5

How Do I Collaborate to Learn Even More?

As a new graduate, I could not help but puff up my chest with the confidence that pure pedagogy was more than enough to make me a master teacher—after all, I had not only a bachelor's degree in education, but also a master's degree in early childhood education and extensive coursework in speech and language pathology. My college program encouraged working on my own and working as quickly as possible. The goal was to buckle down and get into a classroom so that I could make change in the lives of my future students as soon as I could.

In my first year in the classroom, however, I learned that pedagogy and personal drive alone were not enough. I was very fortunate that, in my first year of teaching, I was recruited by a supportive principal to a school with a strong culture of collaboration. This was an adjustment for me—I had always worked alone—but it gave me an opportunity to be reflective and to work through strategies and resources that would most benefit my students during each lesson. During that time, I learned a great deal from planning with my grade-level team.

So far in this book, we've addressed ways you can make sure that your classroom is meeting the strengths and needs of your students. You've used data to understand what your students need. You've matched resources and approaches to those needs. You've tried out those resources and approaches in your classroom, and you've watched the results carefully to determine what to do next. This is a cycle that you can use over and over, and each time you use it, you'll learn more about your students and strengthen your teaching.

However, I would be remiss if I ended the book with only that help. Powerful as that cycle may be, it doesn't take into account one of the most powerful resources you have available to you: your colleagues.

All Hands on Deck!

The first step in effective collaboration is figuring out who to collaborate with. If we want to support the overall growth and success of students, we need to invite all individuals that provide instructional support to students to the planning table. Specialized teachers can give you specific details that general education teachers may not have immediate access to, helping you to quickly individualize support of all of the students in your class. Collaboration among your grade-level team is just as important as collaborating with the special education teacher or gifted teacher. Sharing strategies and resources as a team helps to align the instructional delivery and provide additional practice opportunities that will lead to student progress. (See Figure 5.1.)

Who's Invited to the Planning Table?	
Who Will Support?	**How Can They Help?**
General education teacher	Plan, modify, and evaluate instructional practices, curriculum, and resources used for daily instruction. Coordinate with all individuals that provide instructional support to ensure that the individual needs of each student are being met.
Special education teacher	Adapt lessons to meet the specific needs outlined in a student's Individualized Educational Plan. Discuss strategies and modifications that will help to provide instructional support for special education students.
English Language Learner (ELL) teacher	Provide teachers support to plan, monitor, and assess skills needed for English language proficiency. Identify basic methods and resources needed to increase vocabulary, sentence construction, and reading fluency.
Gifted teacher	Support teachers to plan challenging lessons that extend beyond the general curriculum. Responsible for organizing, implementing, and supporting modified instructional tasks and strategies at student's ability level.
Early Intervention Program (EIP) teacher	Provide additional instructional resources to help students who are performing below grade level obtain the necessary academic skills to reach grade-lèvel performance in the shortest possible time.
Specialty teachers (such as teachers of art, music, or physical education)	Align and enhance lessons to incorporate arts and physical education to foster a creative space where connections across all content areas can be made.
Reading specialists	Provide teachers with additional data points for the students they support. Working with students in a smaller setting allows the reading specialist to suggest additional resources and strategies that could yield student growth throughout their instructional day.
Instructional coaches	Suggest resources and instructional strategies as a result of hearing firsthand about specific students' grade-level needs. Based on common trends, coaches have the ability to support teachers by tailoring activities for individual classrooms or students.
Administrators	Support teachers and instructional coaches by looking through the lens of the school's overall academic vision and ensuring that planning and efforts are aligned to the academic needs of each student.

Figure 5.1 Who's Invited to the Planning Table?

Collaborating with others can give us insights about our students that we could not gain on our own. It can also strengthen the safety net for our students. I recall one of my third graders, Juan. He loved school and was always positive and willing to try new things. One day, Juan was escorted by the principal to my room. The principal said that he was lost and could not remember my name or what grade he was in. Juan and I had been in the same school since he was in first grade! How did this happen? After gathering my thoughts, I had conversations with the special education and ELL teachers and learned, to my surprise, that Juan had fallen through the cracks. He had not been formally evaluated since being retained in kindergarten! Fortunately, I was able to solicit the support of the Early Intervention Program teacher, and with the consent of the parent, we provided him with an additional forty-five minutes of reading and math instruction two times per week. During that time, we began gathering formative and summative assessment data while going through the Response to Intervention process. With help from the Student Support Team, he qualified for the special education program and received proper support and modifications that helped to improve his overall performance.

Collaborating can also help us to better serve entire groups of students. For a few years, my school had an ongoing problem: students who were performing above grade level were not testing into the gifted program. These students were out-of-the-box thinkers, but they had limited experience with project-based learning that tested their critical thinking skills. As a result, my principal developed a team to provide staff with additional resources and professional learning to better equip students that were identified as candidates for this program—not only the gifted education teacher, but also a specialty teacher (in this case, our physical education teacher), a special education teacher, general education teachers, an ELL teacher, an instructional coach, and me (a teacher with a gifted endorsement).

We met each month to discuss ways to incorporate gifted and talent development teaching strategies and resources that could provide additional opportunities for all students to be better equipped for success when testing into the program. Because of our intentional efforts and collaborative efforts, the number of gifted and talent development students increased within the year.

Consider What You Can Accomplish with Collaboration

> Research suggests that collaboration with colleagues around student instruction is an essential part of every teacher's job and results in rising student achievement. (Killough 2011)

Collaboration is about working with individuals to produce, create, or share something: the work must have a focus. Collaboration can be a gift—it can take a heavy load off of one person, and it can bring together individuals with unique expertise. However, without a clear focus, attempts at collaboration can feel purposeless. Here are a few options for ways to focus collaboration with colleagues.

- ***Analyzing the Progression of a Skill or Standard.*** Understanding how a skill progresses within or across grade levels is important when determining the most useful resource to use to adequately address all aspects of grade-level expectations. This supports the teacher with differentiating instruction using best practices.

- ***Considering Options for Remediation of Skills.*** There is not one size fits all for students and that goes for resources as well. Resources can be used in a variety of ways and for a variety of purposes. Sharing these resources and uses among your team can help maximize their impact on your students.
- ***Doing a Deep Dive into Student Work.*** Analyzing student work allows teachers to evaluate the connection between the standard/skill, the instruction, and the assessment. By beginning with the end in mind, teams are able to first identify student strengths, areas for growth, and misconceptions and then consider appropriate resources to address their needs.
- ***Previewing and Trying Out Resources, Strategies, and Manipulatives.*** Teammates can help you to find reliable websites, authors, and resources. Discussing their value for addressing a particular need or building on a clear strength can ensure alignment and appropriateness for the students that will use the resource/manipulatives.
- ***Reviewing Assessment Data.*** Discussing formative and summative assessments with a team gives you an opportunity to compare apples with apples and oranges with oranges when discussing student growth. Misconceptions, strengths, and areas of growth can be identified as a grade-level team and decisions for further or additional instruction can be made. As a team, you become thought partners, and all students benefit from the team's pooled resources and best practices.

Collaborate with the Right Team for Your Purpose

Drawing on all of these experts can be powerful and transformative, as it was for Juan. However, we can also work with a smaller team when we are collaborating for a particular purpose. Although any collaboration regarding resources should include a discussion of the resources, best practice, and assessments, the purpose of the work might be about grade-level consistency, subject-area concerns, or progression of skills across

grades. Each of these different purposes requires a different set of participants. Figure 5.2 helps to provide a framework for things to consider to maintain focus while collaborating with colleagues.

Vertical Planning

Collaborators: Teachers across multiple grade levels

Advantage: Teachers are able to collaborate with teachers from various grades to discuss the use of activities, resources, and best practices for the purpose of improving student performance. During these sessions, teachers are able to discuss misconceptions or foundational skills that are essential to help strengthen students' understanding as they progress through each grade.

Limitations: Discussions are usually general because the grade-specific skills and standards are not being addressed; therefore, teachers will need to allocate additional time to plan for the specific grade-level needs of their students.

Meeting Guide		
Grade Level or Subject		
Type of Planning *(vertical, grade level, subject)*		
Who is involved? *Consider the roles and resources of each individual during the meeting.*		
Session Focus *What focus areas would support student learning during instructional delivery?*		
Objective(s)		**Action Step(s)**
1.		1.
2.		2.
3.		3.
Helpful Resources/Materials *What is needed to complete each action step?*		
Suggest Next Steps *How will the team follow up on the action steps?*		

See Appendix H for a larger copy of the Meeting Guide or download a printable version on the product page on Heinemann's website under Companion Resources (hein.pub/righttools).

Figure 5.2 Meeting Guide

Grade-Level Planning

Collaborators: Teachers on the same grade level

Advantage: Teachers on the same grade level can collaborate to plan, implement, reflect on, and modify instruction. This planning provides opportunities to plan for consistency across the entire grade level. Theme-based teaching can occur by planning cross-curricular lessons that incorporate all content areas. This type of planning helps to support alignment of grade-level activities, assessment, and resources.

Limitations: The extent of this planning can be time-consuming and may not allow all subjects to be adequately discussed in one session. As a result, additional time must be scheduled to discuss resources, strategies, misconceptions, and so on.

Subject Alike Planning

Collaborators: Teachers of the same content area

Advantage: Teachers are able to plan for instruction for each content area. This type of planning may cross various grade levels, but teachers discuss a variety of resources, best practices, and strategies that can support students with a conceptual understanding of the subject matter. Resources are more specific to each content area and can be used to explicitly reinforce the student's understanding of the material.

Limitations: Similar-subject teachers may not have an understanding that other contents areas can help to reinforce the subject being planned. There may be limited experience in the use of specific resources from other content areas and how they can strengthen the content-specific activities. During this type of planning, content teachers could often feel like they are the sole providers of information on the subject matter and do not benefit from the sharing of resources and best practices through collaboration with other content teachers.

Collaborating with Your Team Gives You Access to More Resources!

My first year as a teacher is a good reminder of just how isolated we educators can be in our classrooms. I spent much of my first few paychecks on decor to make my room look inviting. However, as I began meeting with my team members, they began to challenge my priorities. Instead of emphasizing only the room's appearance, they opened my eyes to how the physical classroom space could support learning with literacy centers, independent reading, and the workshop model of instruction. It was the influence of my team, not my classroom decor, that gave my students a true learning environment.

Share strategies and resources like food during a holiday gathering.

Don't be shy about recommending resources, sharing strategies, or asking for resource suggestions. (Sharing snacks doesn't hurt, either!)

My grade-level teams used our time together to consider how specific lessons might work with our students, and we made modifications—adding opportunities to build background knowledge, sharing videos or photographs to augment lessons, offering whatever we could to help each other be intentional with our lessons—prior to using the lessons with our students.

Try out strategies and resources with your team first.

If you've ever muttered, "That's not how I learned it" to yourself when looking at an educational resource, you know that education is ever evolving. It's not uncommon for us to have learned concepts differently from the way students learn them today. You might, as some of my grade-level teams have done, conduct "teach backs": literally using the materials and resources to teach the lesson, with the team acting as the students, and calling attention to possible misconceptions or potential difficulties in the lesson. We did the heavy lifting as a team before we taught the lessons in our classrooms, which helped us to anticipate where to place most of our effort in the lesson.

Learn from other educators.

I was fortunate to have an awesome mentor teacher my first few years of teaching. I remember planning after school so that I could sit in the back of her class and observe the routines, procedures, resources, and strategies that she used with her students, during my planning time.

Learning to teach does not stop once you have your diploma, or even an advanced degree. A mentor might be someone you observe, as I did with mine, or someone you visit to discuss a particular issue. You might even ask a mentor to observe a lesson in your classroom to help you better understand how your students are responding to it. Any time that you would benefit from a new perspective or fresh ideas, you can turn to a mentor. There are so many educators who are willing to share ideas and challenge your way of teaching. We can keep learning from colleagues in person in our own schools or across states, countries, and even continents, thanks to social media.

Always Keep Learning

As teachers, there will always be factors that are outside our sphere of influence: the school's demographics, the state curriculum, and school staffing, to name a few. There may even be times when available resources, professional development training, and parental involvement may feel beyond our ability to change. However, we always have the opportunity to keep learning. In truth, we have a *responsibility* to keep learning, because in each class, students will have different strengths and needs. When our learning stops, our teaching stops.

Professional learning can take different forms: It might be a workshop that is required by your district or school. It might be your own self-directed, self-monitored growth, drawing from connections you make online or on social media as well as from any professional books, workshops, or webinars you choose. Or, it might be a professional learning community (PLC).

A PLC is just what its name implies: a community of people who are focused on professional learning. Although the term *professional learning community* may mean slightly different things to different people, I agree with Solution Tree's definition of PLCs: "an ongoing process in which educators work collaboratively in recurring cycles of collective inquiry and action research to achieve better results for the students they serve" (*All Things PLC* 2018).

- ***A strong PLC has a focus on learning.*** Discussions and work are centered around ensuring that all students are learning. The work within these sessions is goal-oriented and allows for accountability markers to monitor the success of teachers' efforts.
- ***A strong PLC inquires into best practices.*** PLCs allow educators to learn about best practices in teaching and learning. This safe space gives educators opportunities to reflect on their personal current practices and the direct impact of those practices on their students' learning. They are able to ask teammates probing and guiding questions that attempt to build upon their knowledge rather than simply pooling individual opinions together.

- ***A strong PLC supports learning by doing.*** I heard a principal say, "Work out the kinks before you get in front of students." A PLC gives educators an opportunity to do just that. Being able to work through activities with colleagues helps to identify possible misconceptions or questions that students may have during the learning experience.
- ***A strong PLC is committed to continuous improvement.*** As one superintendent explains, "The goal [of professional learning] is not simply to learn a new strategy, but instead to create conditions for a perpetual learning environment in which innovation and experimentation are viewed not as tasks to be accomplished or projects to be completed but as ways of conducting day-to-day business—forever" (Richards 2017, 14–15). When teachers in a PLC are continuously analyzing student work, they are ensuring alignment between formative/summative assessments and delivery of instruction, and they can apply their new learning about best practices to address their students' needs and strengths.

Conversation Starters

Colleagues, instructional coaches, and administrators can be valuable resources for ideas and feedback as you plan how you'll use new resources and approaches. A few questions might lead to helpful discussions:

- How have you seen the use of collaborative planning support teachers with improving student performance?
- How might the ELL, special education, and gifted teachers be a resource to provide additional support in my classroom?
- What are the aims of our school-based and district-based professional learning opportunities? What other opportunities for professional learning are available? What funding for additional professional learning is available?
- How does our school's or district's current professional growth focus align with my work in my classroom? How does it benefit my students?

Putting It into Practice

While writing this book, I reflected back on the progression of learning in my own journey as an educator. I have had the privilege of looking at education through the school, district, and even the state lens. Time and time again, in each of the roles I've held, I have seen students respond positively when a teacher is intentional about what he or she places before them.

Every opportunity that we have with our students is an opportunity to stretch their thinking. Providing research-based resources and best practices aligned with what our students need from us fosters an environment for real learning, in which students are doing the heavy lifting. Because, as we know, when we do most of the talking, then we (not our students) do most of the learning.

Every suggestion, example, chart, and checklist within this book points back to your students. As the experts who are entrusted with our students' learning, we must be protective of the children in our care, always asking ourselves, "What's working? What's not working?"

Thank you for joining me on this journey as we all strive to do what's best for all students.

Appendixes

Student Progress Tracker

Academic Achievement (*Beginner*–**B**, *Developing*–**De**, *Proficient*–**P**, *Distinguished*–**D**)

Name:	**Reading Comprehension**			**Fluency**			**Phonics (K–2 only)**			**Reading Level**		
	Fall	Winter	Spring	Fall	Winter	Spring	Fall	Winter	Spring	Fall	Winter	Spring
	Strengths:			Strengths:			Strengths:			Additional Comments:		
	Needs:			Needs:			Needs:					
Name:	**Reading Comprehension**			**Fluency**			**Phonics (K–2 only)**			**Reading Level**		
	Fall	Winter	Spring	Fall	Winter	Spring	Fall	Winter	Spring	Fall	Winter	Spring
	Strengths:			Strengths:			Strengths:			Additional Comments:		
	Needs:			Needs:			Needs:					
Name:	**Reading Comprehension**			**Fluency**			**Phonics (K–2 only)**			**Reading Level**		
	Fall	Winter	Spring	Fall	Winter	Spring	Fall	Winter	Spring	Fall	Winter	Spring
	Strengths:			Strengths:			Strengths:			Additional Comments:		
	Needs:			Needs:			Needs:					

<table>
<tr><th colspan="14">Student Progress Tracker</th></tr>
<tr><th>Student</th><th colspan="9">Academic Achievement (Beginner–B, Developing–De, Proficient–P, Distinguished–D)</th><th colspan="4">Instructional Support
(Mark all that apply)</th></tr>
<tr><td rowspan="4">Name:</td><td colspan="3">Vocabulary</td><td colspan="3">Response to Reading</td><td colspan="3">Writing</td><td>ELL</td><td>EIP</td><td>IEP</td><td>Gifted</td></tr>
<tr><td>Fall</td><td>Winter</td><td>Spring</td><td>Fall</td><td>Winter</td><td>Spring</td><td>Fall</td><td>Winter</td><td>Spring</td><td></td><td></td><td></td><td></td></tr>
<tr><td colspan="3">Strengths:</td><td colspan="3">Strengths:</td><td colspan="3">Strengths:</td><td colspan="4" rowspan="2">Notes/Accommodations:</td></tr>
<tr><td colspan="3">Needs:</td><td colspan="3">Needs:</td><td colspan="3">Needs:</td></tr>
<tr><td rowspan="4">Name:</td><td colspan="3">Vocabulary</td><td colspan="3">Response to Reading</td><td colspan="3">Writing</td><td>ELL</td><td>EIP</td><td>IEP</td><td>Gifted</td></tr>
<tr><td>Fall</td><td>Winter</td><td>Spring</td><td>Fall</td><td>Winter</td><td>Spring</td><td>Fall</td><td>Winter</td><td>Spring</td><td></td><td></td><td></td><td></td></tr>
<tr><td colspan="3">Strengths:</td><td colspan="3">Strengths:</td><td colspan="3">Strengths:</td><td colspan="4" rowspan="2">Notes/Accommodations:</td></tr>
<tr><td colspan="3">Needs:</td><td colspan="3">Needs:</td><td colspan="3">Needs:</td></tr>
<tr><td rowspan="4">Name:</td><td colspan="3">Vocabulary</td><td colspan="3">Response to Reading</td><td colspan="3">Writing</td><td>ELL</td><td>EIP</td><td>IEP</td><td>Gifted</td></tr>
<tr><td>Fall</td><td>Winter</td><td>Spring</td><td>Fall</td><td>Winter</td><td>Spring</td><td>Fall</td><td>Winter</td><td>Spring</td><td></td><td></td><td></td><td></td></tr>
<tr><td colspan="3">Strengths:</td><td colspan="3">Strengths:</td><td colspan="3">Strengths:</td><td colspan="4" rowspan="2">Notes/Accommodations:</td></tr>
<tr><td colspan="3">Needs:</td><td colspan="3">Needs:</td><td colspan="3">Needs:</td></tr>
</table>

Student Progress Descriptors

Some behaviors to look for . . .

	Beginner	Developing	Proficient
Reading Comprehension	Students cannot engage with the text and struggle with keeping a constant check on their understanding of the text. They do not stop to use a "figure-it-out" strategy when they do not understand what they read. They do not look for important ideas and do not see how details relate to the whole. They rarely show evidence of making inferences and connections in their reading.	Students struggle with engaging in the text and inconsistently keep a check on their understanding of the text. They are inconsistent when stopping to use a "figure-it-out" strategy when they do not understand what they read. They seldom show evidence of looking for important ideas and seldom see how details relate to the whole. They sometimes show evidence of making inferences and connections in their reading.	Students are engaged in the text by keeping a constant check on their understanding of the text. They stop to use a "figure-it-out" strategy when they do not understand what they read. They look for important ideas and see how details relate to the whole. The students show evidence of making inferences and connections as they read.
Comments			
Fluency	Students are not confident in their understandings of text while reading independently. The students' struggle with maintaining meaning through longer and more complex stretches of language is not grade-level appropriate. While reading, students have difficulty paying attention to details and reading with accuracy, proper expression, and proper volume.	Students are inconsistently confident in their understandings of text while reading independently. The students' ability to maintain meaning through longer and more complex stretches of language is somewhat grade-level appropriate. While reading, students sometimes are able to pay attention to details and read with accuracy, proper expression, and proper volume.	Students are consistently confident in their understandings of text while reading independently. The students' competence in maintaining meaning through longer and more complex stretches of language is grade-level appropriate. While reading, students pay attention to details and show accuracy, proper expression, and proper volume.
Comments			
Phonics (K–2)	Students do not display an understanding of the predictable relationship between the sounds of spoken language and the letters and spellings that represent those sounds in written language. The students struggle with grade-appropriate decoding and do not use their knowledge of letter-sound relationships accurately to read a word.	Students display some understanding of the predictable relationship between the sounds of spoken language and the letters and spellings that represent those sounds in written language. The students struggle with decoding but somewhat use their knowledge of letter–sound relationships accurately to read a word.	Students display a strong understanding that there is a predictable relationship between the sounds of spoken language and the letters and spellings that represent those sounds in written language. The students are able to decode using their knowledge of letter-sound relationships accurately to read a word.
Comments			

Student Progress Descriptors

Some behaviors to look for . . .

	Beginner	Developing	Proficient
Vocabulary	Students do not use word-meaning strategies. They do not use context to determine a word's meaning or to make sense of text.	Students use word-meaning strategies inconsistently. They sometimes use context to determine a word's meaning or to make sense of the text.	Students consistently use word-meaning strategies. They use context to determine a word's meaning or to make sense of the text.
Comments			
Response to Reading	Students' responses are not organized, and their summaries are vague. Their opinions and inferences are not supported by evidence from the text. Their responses do not make connections to other text, the world, or their own experiences.	Students' responses are somewhat organized, and their summaries are vague. Their opinions and inferences are loosely supported by evidence from the text. Their responses partially make connections to other text, the world, or their own experiences.	Students' responses are organized, accurately summarize the text, and include opinions or inferences that are supported by evidence from the text. Their responses make connections to other text, the world, or their own experiences.
Comments			
Writing	The students do not express their ideas clearly in writing. Their writing is disorganized or illogical, ineffectively communicating the writers' thoughts. Students' use of voice is not appropriate to the purpose and audience. Their word choices are not meaningful. They struggle with exhibiting strong convention skills. Their sentence fluency is not smooth and expressive.	The students somewhat express their ideas clearly in writing. Their ideas may be vague or in need of clearer organization. Their writing communicates the writers' thoughts somewhat. The students' use of voice, word choice, conventions, and sentence fluency is somewhat developed and appropriate to the purpose and audience.	The students express their ideas clearly in writing. The writing is logical, is well organized, and effectively communicates the writers' thoughts. Students' use of voice is appropriate to the purpose and audience, and their word choices are specific and meaningful. They exhibit strong convention skills and their sentence fluency is smooth and expressive.
Comments			

Appendix C Student Self-Reflection Checklist

Student Self-Reflection Checklist				
Reading Comprehension				
As I read, I continue to check for understanding.				
I stop to use a reading strategy when I do not understand what I read.				
I look for important ideas and see how the details in the text relate to the whole.				
I can visualize in my head the events noted in the text.				
I can make connections to the text to make an inference.				

Student Self-Reflection Checklist	
Fluency	
I am confident in my understandings of text and how text works.	
I can read the text independently.	
I use strategies to help me read words aloud and maintain meaning of sentences or paragraphs.	
As I read, I pay attention to details and read every word.	
I can show proper expression and use proper volume as I read.	

Student Self-Reflection Checklist	
Phonics (K-2)	
I can sound out one-syllable words with short- and long-vowel spellings.	
I can segment, or separate, a word sound by sound.	
I understand how changing letters in a word changes the sounds and the meaning.	
I can blend individual letter sounds together to form a word.	
I can decode words by identifying the spelling patterns.	

Student Self-Reflection Checklist				
Vocabulary				
I can identify word parts to understand the meaning of unknown words.				
I use word-meaning strategies to understand important ideas.				
I know how to connect an individual word meaning to the overall meaning of an entire text.				
I understand meaning in context by using information surrounding each new word to determine how it is being used.				
I am able to infer the meaning of new words while reading to ensure that the text makes sense.				

Student Self-Reflection Checklist				
Response to Reading				
I can express my ideas in writing, using important key information that connects to a specific topic.				
My ideas are original, and I utilize the text as a reference to support my ideas within my writing.				
I organize my writing in an order that communicates my thoughts.				
My writing voice is appropriate, and my word choice is specific and meaningful.				
I exhibit strong convention skills, and my sentence fluency is smooth and expressive.				

Student Self-Reflection Checklist	
Writing	
I understand the purpose of this type of writing is to respond to information or key details in a piece of informational or literary text.	
I can write a response to a piece of text.	
I can summarize the text.	
My opinion is supported by evidence from the text.	
I can make connections to the text by making connections to other texts, the world, or my experiences.	

Goal Setting: Tracking Achievements							
What's Your *Reading* Goal?	Benchmark	Fall	Goal Met?	Winter	Goal Met?	Spring	Goal Met?

To meet my goal, I will . . .

- ______________________________
- ______________________________
- ______________________________

Goal Setting: Tracking Achievements							
What's Your *Writing* Goal?	Benchmark	Fall	Goal Met?	Winter	Goal Met?	Spring	Goal Met?

To meet my goal, I will . . .

- ______________________________
- ______________________________
- ______________________________

Appendix E Resource Inventory Checklist

Resource Inventory Checklist																			
	Stages			**Skill(s)** (needs you identified in Chapter 1)				**Grouping**				**Expected Outcomes**				**Depth of Knowledge**			
Resources	I do	You do	We do					Whole Group	Small Group	One on One	Independent	Exposure	Remediation of Skills	Mastery (assessment)	Practice Opportunities	Level 1: Recall and Reproduction*	Level 2: Skills and Concepts**	Level 3: Strategic Thinking***	Level 4: Extended Thinking****

(Copy or print additional pages as necessary)

* Recalling facts and simple procedures

** Deciding on an approach to solving a problem

*** Abstract thinking/Using planning and evidence to complete a task

**** Synthesizing information; transferring knowledge from one domain to another

Unpacking the Standards

Grade	
Standard/Skill	
Verbs	**Nouns**
Students will be able to: What skills should students practice?	
In order to: What higher-level skill does this support?	
Academic Vocabulary: What skill-/standard-specific words will students need to know?	
Suggested Activities	**Helpful Resources/Materials**

Appendix G Grouping Planner

Grouping Planner		
Academic Purpose/Goal:		
Decisions to Be Made	**Options**	**How This Plan Benefits Your Students**
Who will choose the groups?	☐ Teacher ☐ Students	
If the groups are teacher chosen, how will they be determined?	☐ Academically homogeneous (grouped by goal or by readiness/skill level) ☐ Academically heterogeneous (grouped by learning style, interest, or some other characteristic)	
How big will the groups be?	☐ Partners (2 students) ☐ Triad (3 students) ☐ Small group (4–5 students) ☐ Split class	
How will the groups use class time?	• Frequency of meetings: ☐ Single meeting ☐ Multiple meetings over a few days ☐ Multiple meetings for more than a week • Length of each meeting: ☐ Less than one class period ☐ One class period	
How will the groups be flexible?	☐ Whole class ☐ Small group ☐ Partner	

Appendix H Meeting Guide

Meeting Guide		
Grade Level or Subject		
Type of Planning (*vertical, grade level, subject*)		
Who is involved? *Consider the roles and resources of each individual during the meeting.*		
Session Focus *What focus areas would support student learning during instructional delivery?*		
Objective(s)		**Action Step(s)**
1. 2. 3.		1. 2. 3.
Helpful Resources/Materials *What is needed to complete each action step?*		
Suggest Next Steps *How will the team follow up on the action steps?*		

References

All Things PLC (blog). 2018. Solution Tree, Inc. www.allthingsplc.info/about.

Beck, Isabel L., Margaret M. McKeown, and Linda Kucan. 2013. *Bringing Words to Life: Robust Vocabulary Instruction*, 2nd ed. New York: Guilford Press.

Dewitz, Peter, and Jonni Wolskee. 2012. *Making the Most of Your Core Reading Program: Research-Based Essentials*. Portsmouth, NH: Heinemann.

Dufour, Richard. 2010. *Learning by Doing: A Handbook for Professional Learning Communities at Work*. Bloomington, IN: Solution Tree Press.

Duke, Nell, and P. David Pearson. 2002. *What Research Has to Say About Reading Instruction*, 3rd ed. Newark, DE: International Literacy Association.

Elmore, Richard F. 2008. "Improving the Instructional Core." Unpublished manuscript, rev. 6/2008.

Fisher, Douglas. 2008. "Effective Use of the Gradual Release of Responsibility Model." Author Monographs. *Treasures*. www.mheonline.com/_treasures/pdf/douglas_fisher.pdf. New York: Macmillan/McGraw-Hill.

Gottlieb, Margo H., and Gisela Ernst-Slavit. 2013. *Academic Language in Diverse Classrooms: Mathematics, Grades 3–5. Promoting Content and Language Learning*. Thousand Oaks, CA: Corwin.

Gronlund, Norman E. 2005. *Assessment of Student Achievement*, 8th ed. Boston: Allyn & Bacon.

Institute of Education Sciences. *What Works Clearinghouse Standards Handbook*, Version 4.0. https://ies.ed.gov/ncee/wwc/Docs/referenceresources/wwc_standards_handbook_v4.pdf.

Kamil, Michael L., P. David Pearson, Elizabeth Birr Moje, and Peter P. Afflerbach. 2011. *Handbook of Reading Research*, Vol. 4. New York: Routledge.

Killough, Laurel. 2011. "Research Shows Teacher Collaboration Helps Raise Student Achievement." *BlogCEA*, September 30. blogcea.org/2011/09/30/collaboration-raises-achievement/.

Linder, Rozlyn. 2014a. *Chart Sense: Common Sense Charts to Teach 3–8 Informational Text and Literature*. Atlanta: The Literacy Initiative.

———. 2014b. *K–2 Chart Sense: Common Sense Charts to Teach K–2 Informational Text and Literature*. Atlanta: The Literacy Initiative.

———. 2016. *The Big Book of Details: 46 Moves for Teaching Writers to Elaborate*. Portsmouth, NH: Heinemann.

McKenna, Michael C., and Katherine A. Dougherty Stahl. 2015. *Assessment for Reading Instruction*. New York: Guilford Press.

Richards, I. 2017. *Professional Learning Plan*. Greenwood, MS: Leflore County School District. https://bit.ly/2QgkKGH.

Richardson, Jan. 2013a. *Next Step Guided Reading in Action: Grades 3–6*. New York: Scholastic Teaching Resources.

——— 2013b. *Next Step Guided Reading in Action: View & Do Guide*. New York: Scholastic.

———. 2016. *The Next Step Forward in Guided Reading: An Assess-Decide-Guide Framework for Supporting Every Reader*. New York: Scholastic.

Serravallo, Jennifer. 2015. *The Reading Strategies Book: Your Everything Guide to Developing Skilled Readers*. Portsmouth, NH: Heinemann.

———. 2017. *The Writing Strategies Book: Your Everything Guide to Developing Skilled Writers*. Portsmouth, NH: Heinemann.

Smith, Nila B. 1986. *American Reading Instruction*. Newark, DE: International Reading Association.

Walpole, Sharon, and Michael C. McKenna. 2017. *How to Plan Differentiated Reading Instruction: Resources for Grades K–3*. New York: Guilford Press.

Walpole, Sharon, Michael C. McKenna, and Zoi A. Philippakos. 2011. *Differentiated Reading Instruction in Grades 4 and 5: Strategies and Resources*. New York: Guilford Press.